International Labour and Employment Compliance Handbook

www.kluwerlawonline.com

Labour and Employment Compliance in France

International Bar Association

Labour and Employment Compliance in France

Fifth Edition

Pascale Lagesse

This publication is part of the International Labour
and Employment Compliance Handbook,
available on www.kluwerlawonline.com

Editors: Salvador del Rey and Robert J. Mignin

the global voice of
the legal profession

Wolters Kluwer

Published by:
Kluwer Law International B.V.
PO Box 316
2400 AH Alphen aan den Rijn
The Netherlands
Website: www.wolterskluwerlr.com

Sold and distributed in North, Central and South America by:
Wolters Kluwer Legal & Regulatory U.S.
7201 McKinney Circle
Frederick, MD 21704
United States of America
Email: customer.service@wolterskluwer.com

Sold and distributed in all other countries by:
Quadrant
Rockwood House
Haywards Heath
West Sussex
RH16 3DH
United Kingdom
Email: international-customerservice@wolterskluwer.com

Printed on acid-free paper.

ISBN 978-90-411-9319-3

e-Book: ISBN 978-90-411-9351-3
web-PDF: ISBN 978-90-411-9383-4

Printed and Bound by CPI Group (UK) Ltd, Croydon, CR0 4YY.

FSC
MIX
FSC® C103993

All listed titles are also available on lrus.wolterskluwer.com

1. Argentina: Julio César Stefanoni Zani & Enrique Alfredo Betemps, *Labour and Employment Compliance in Argentina, 5th edition*, 2017 (ISBN 978-90-411-9316-2)
2. Australia: John Tuck, Stephen Price, Rosemary Roach, Jack de Flamingh, Nicholas Ellery & Nick Le Mare, *Labour and Employment Compliance in Australia, 2nd edition*, 2016 (ISBN 978-90-411-8493-1)
3. Belgium: Chris Van Olmen, *Labour and Employment Compliance in Belgium, 2nd edition*, 2017 (978-90411-9329-2)
4. Brazil: Rodrigo Seizo Takano, Andrea Giamondo Massei Rossi & Murilo Caldeira Germiniani, *Labour and Employment Compliance in Brazil, 4th edition*, 2017 (ISBN 978-90-411-9330-8)
5. Canada: Kevin Coon & Adrian Ishak, *Labour and Employment Compliance in Canada, 2nd edition*, 2014 (ISBN 978-90-411-5637-2)
6. Chile: Gerardo Otero A., Maria Dolores Echeverria F., Macarena López M.& María de los Ángeles Fernández S., *Labour and Employment Compliance in Chile, 5th edition*, 2017 (ISBN 978-90-411-9317-9)
7. China: King & Wood Mallesons, *Labour and Employment Compliance in China, 4th edition*, 2017 (ISBN 978-90-411-9318-6)
8. England: Tony Hyams-Parish, *Labour and Employment Compliance in England, 5th edition*, 2017 (ISBN 978-90-411-9337-7)
9. France: Pascale Lagesse, *Labour and Employment Compliance in France, 5th edition*, 2017 (ISBN 978-90411-9319-3)
10. Germany: Gerlind Wisskirchen & Martin Lützeler, *Labour and Employment Compliance in Germany, 5th edition*, 2017 (ISBN 978-90-411-9323-0)
11. India: Manishi Pathak, *Labour and Employment Compliance in India, 4th edition*, 2016 (ISBN 978-90-411-8496-2)
12. Ireland: Duncan Inverarity & Sinead Grace, *Labour and Employment Compliance in Ireland, 3rd edition*, 2016 (ISBN 978-90-411-8751-2)
13. Israel: Yaron Horovitz, Pnina Broder-Manor & Helen Raziel, *Labour and Employment Compliance in Israel, 4th edition*, 2017 (ISBN 978-90411-9320-9)
14. Italy: Angelo Zambelli, *Labour and Employment Compliance in Italy, 5th edition*, 2017 (ISBN 97890-411-9321-6)
15. Japan: Yoshikazu Sugino, *Labour and Employment Compliance in Japan, 5th edition*, 2017 (ISBN 978-90-411-9324-7)
16. Republic of Korea: Sang Wook Cho, Soojung Lee & Christopher Mandel, *Labour and Employment Compliance in the Republic of Korea*, 3rd edition, 2017 (ISBN 978-90-411-9325-4)
17. Mexico: Oscar De La Vega Gómez, *Labour and Employment Compliance in Mexico, 5th edition*, 2017 (ISBN 978-90-411-9333-9)
18. The Netherlands: Els de Wind & Cara Pronk, *Labour and Employment Compliance in the Netherlands, 2nd edition*, 2016 (ISBN 978-90-411-8498-6)
19. Poland: Barbara Jóźwik, *Labour and Employment Compliance in Poland, 5th edition*, 2017 (ISBN 978-90-411-9326-1)

20. Russia: Anna-Stefaniya Chepik, *Labour and Employment Compliance in Russia*, 2013 (ISBN 978-90-411-4925-1).
21. South Africa: Susan Stelzner, Stuart Harrison, Brian Patterson & Zahida Ebrahim, *Labour and Employment Compliance in South Africa, 5th edition*, 2017 (ISBN 978-90-411-9327-8)
22. Spain: Salvador del Rey & Ana Campos, *Labour and Employment Compliance in Spain, 5th edition*, 2017 (978-90411-9335-3)
23. Turkey: Nuri Bodur, Elif Nur Çakir & Ozan Kesim, *Labour and Employment Compliance in Turkey, 2nd edition*, 2016 (ISBN 978-90-411-8492-4)
24. United Arab Emirates: Sara Khoja & Sarit Thomas, *Labour and Employment Compliance in the United Arab Emirates, 3rd edition*, 2016 (ISBN 978-90-411-8500-6)
25. United States: Baker & McKenzie LLP, *Labour and Employment Compliance in the United States, 3rd edition*, 2015 (ISBN 978-90-411-6256-4)

International Bar Association
The Global Voice of the Legal Profession

The International Bar Association (IBA), established in 1947, is the world's leading organization of international legal practitioners, bar associations and law societies. The IBA influences the development of international law reform and shapes the future of the legal profession throughout the world. It has a membership of over 40,000 individual lawyers and almost 200 bar associations and law societies spanning all continents. It has considerable expertise in providing assistance to the global legal community.

Grouped into two divisions – the Legal Practice Division and the Public and Professional Interest Division – the IBA covers all practice areas and professional interests, providing members with access to leading experts and up-to-date information. Through the various committees of the divisions, the IBA enables an interchange of information and views among its members as to laws, practices and professional responsibilities relating to the practice of business law around the globe. Additionally, the IBA's high-quality publications and world-class conferences provide unrivalled professional development and network-building opportunities for international legal practitioners and professional associates.

The IBA's Bar Issues Commission provides an invaluable forum for IBA member organisations to discuss all matters relating to law at an international level.

The IBA's Human Rights Institute (IBAHRI) works across the Association, to promote, protect and enforce human rights under a just rule of law, and to preserve the independence of the judiciary and the legal profession worldwide.

Other institutions established by the IBA include the Southern Africa Litigation Centre and the International Legal Assistance Consortium.

Employment and Industrial Relations Law Committee

The aims of the committee are to develop and exchange knowledge of employment and industrial relations law and practice. Members support each other through the provision of innovative ideas and practical assistance on day-to-day issues. In addition, through its journal and through presentations, conferences, the committee ensures the dissemination of up-to-date law and practice in this highly important business area.

International Bar Association Global Employment Institute

The IBA Global Employment Institute (IBA GEI) was formed in early 2010 for the purpose of developing for multinationals and worldwide institutions a global and strategic approach to the key legal issues in the human resources and human capital fields.

Drawing on the resources and expertise of the IBA membership, the IBA GEI will provide a unique contribution in the field of employment, discrimination and immigration law, on a diverse range of global issues, to private and public organizations throughout the world. The IBA GEI is designed to enhance the management, performance and productivity of these organizations and help achieve best practice in their human capital and management functions from a strategic perspective.

The IBA GEI will become the leading voice and authority on global HR issues by virtue of having a number of the world's leading labour and employment practitioners in its ranks, and the support and resource of the world's largest association of international lawyers.

Further information

International Bar Association, 4th Floor, 10 St Bride Street, London EC4A 4AD, United Kingdom, Tel: +44 (0)20 7842 0090, Fax: +44 (0)20 7842 0091, E-mail: member@int-bar.org, www.ibanet.org

About the International Labour and Employment Compliance Handbook

From 1976 through 1988, the International Bar Association and Kluwer Law International published the groundbreaking International Handbook on Contracts of Employment. This Handbook provided one of the first global overviews of the law of the international employment relationship.

Since publishing the first edition, globalization of business has created an increased demand for knowledge of labor and employment laws throughout the world. Therefore, along with Kluwer, we decided to publish an updated Handbook which we have titled the International Labour and Employment Compliance Handbook.

This new Handbook was intended to be a practical guide by providing a general overview of key labor and employment issues in multiple jurisdictions. Each chapter was written so that it is easy to understand by lawyers and non-lawyers alike. Each country author has also followed a standard outline to assist readers in analysing employment issues in each country.

The first edition of this new Handbook included nineteen (19) different countries.

This Handbook would not have been possible without the help and assistance of many people. Most importantly, the individual country authors are all distinguished legal practitioners who spent considerable time drafting and revising their country reports to meet difficult deadlines. We thank each of them. Our friends at Kluwer, especially Ewa Szkatula, have done a wonderful job in keeping the editors and the authors on schedule. Finally, we want to also express our gratitude to Cuatrecasas, Gonçalves Pereira, and Baker & McKenzie LLP for their valuable assistance in the coordination and organization of this project. Our warmest thanks to each of them.

Because of the success of the Handbook, Wolters Kluwer Law & Business decided to publish each country report also as a separate book to give a choice in obtaining the information. We hope this new format will be a helpful and useful resource just like the Handbook. Both formats are available in print and online.

The Editors

Salvador del Rey Guanter
Robert J. Mignin

March 2013

France

AUTHOR

Pascale Lagesse

Pascale Lagesse is a Partner at Bredin Prat specialising in all aspects of employment law, including national, international and multi-jurisdictional issues. She has extensive experience with complex reorganizations and international restructuring operations, including advising companies on how to plan for and carry out reductions in force and how to best manage the employment issues that arise in connection with mergers and acquisitions, such as works council information/consultation requirements, transfers of undertakings, harmonization of employee benefits and other cross-border arrangements.

Mrs Lagesse was elected to the National Bar Council of France in 2005. She studied law at the University of Paris II (*Maîtrise Carrières Judiciaires*) and Paris I (*DEA en Droit Privé*). She lectures frequently in France and abroad on a wide range of employment-related topics.

Mrs Lagesse is active in a variety of legal organizations. She is the Co-Chair of the IBA Global Employment Institute, a member of the IBA LPD Council and a Member of Best Lawyer's Advisory Board. She served as Chair of the IBA's Employment and Industrial Relations Law Committee from 2009 to 2011.

ADDRESS

Bredin Prat
53 Quai d'Orsay
75007 Paris
France

Tel.: +33 1 44 35 35 35
Fax: +33 1 42 89 10 73
E-mail: pascalelagesse@bredinprat.com
Web: <www.bredinprat.com>

Table of Contents

Legal Compliance in France

1. LEGAL FRAMEWORK: EMPLOYMENT LAWS

1.1. OVERVIEW

In addition to international and European legal sources of labour and employment law, French labour and employment law is based, on the one hand, on State-level sources (the French Constitution, written labour laws and case law) and, on the other hand, on professional sources (collective bargaining agreements, unilateral undertakings by the employer, company practices).

1.2. STATE-LEVEL SOURCES

1.2.1. The French Constitution

The preamble to the French Constitution dated 4 October 1958 sets out a number of principles that apply in labour and employment law: equal rights granted to women and men, the right to employment and non-discrimination, trade union rights and freedoms, the right to strike, employees' participation in the establishment of their working conditions and in the management of the company, vocational training, replacement income.

These principles constitute established and binding standards in France.

1.2.2. Laws and Regulations

Most labour and employment laws and regulations are codified in the French Labour Code.

French labour and employment law is divided into two main branches: rules concerning the employees as individuals and rules concerning employees as a collective group.

The rules concerning employees individually include provisions governing an employee's employment contract, recruitment, career development, salary, transfer and departure (resignation, dismissal, acknowledgement of termination, retirement, etc.). The rules concerning employees collectively include all of the provisions governing the status of employees as a collective group, whether in relation to employee representative bodies, collective bargaining agreements or industrial action.

1.2.3.   Case Law

Case law is the interpretation that judges give to laws and regulations. Labour and employment case law is composed of decisions rendered by jurisdictions such as the French Constitutional Council (*Conseil Constitutionnel*), the French Court of Cassation (*Cour de Cassation*), the French Administrative Supreme Court (*Conseil d'Etat*), courts of appeal (*cours d'appel*) or employment tribunals (*conseils de prud'hommes*).

Through their decisions, the judges participate in creating employment rules.

1.3.   PROFESSIONAL SOURCES

Professional sources include:

– *Collective bargaining agreements*: company-wide, industry-wide and national inter-professional-wide collective agreements.
– *Company practices*: an informal way of establishing employment rules resulting from a repeated practice showing the employer's implicit will to grant benefits to their employees.
– *Unilateral commitments on the part of the employer*: an express decision by the employer to grant benefits to their employees.
– *Special agreements (accords atypiques)*: these can be concluded between the employer and the employees or the staff representatives outside of collective bargaining.
– *Proposals made by employers' organizations to their members.*

1.4. HIERARCHY OF THE DIFFERENT LEVELS OF EMPLOYMENT RULES

The hierarchy of the different sources of French law also applies to labour law rules. Nevertheless, the following trends are worth noting regarding the allocation of roles between notably the law and collective bargaining agreements:

– Court decisions refer increasingly to constitutional, European and international rules.
– Some legal rules are mandatory, that is, they cannot be derogated from even if the result is more advantageous for the employees. For example, this includes rules regarding the termination of employment contracts,[1] the terms of office of employee representatives, trade union freedoms and the payment of remuneration.
– Other legal rules enable the collective bargaining agreements to derogate from the law in specific areas (i.e., working time and 'precarious' employment contracts), regardless of whether or not the provisions are more advantageous for the employees. In such a case, the law simply provides a legal framework which will apply if there is no collective agreement providing otherwise.
– The importance of collective bargaining agreements has dramatically increased in France, especially within the framework of the 2016 labour law reform. Indeed, the structure of the French Labour Code has been substantially amended, specifically setting out provisions enabling company-wide or industry-wide agreements to depart from the law even if the negotiated provisions are less favourable for employees (except for mandatory provisions that may not be departed from). Even if this new presentation is, for the moment, limited to provisions regarding working time, it is intended to be extended to all matters addressed by the Labour Code.

2. RECRUITING, INTERVIEWING, SCREENING AND HIRING EMPLOYEES

2.1. OVERVIEW

In principle, employers are free to choose their employees.

2.2. RECRUITING

Before beginning the hiring process, an employer should establish a set of requirements and standards for the job. An employer can use these requirements

---

1. Employment Chamber of the Court of Cassation, 12 Nov. 2002, *no. 99-45821.*

and standards to compare applicants and decide, based on their skills, experience and background, which candidate should be offered the job.

Pursuant to section L. 1221-8 of the French Labour Code, potential employers must inform candidates in advance of the recruitment methods and techniques that will be used as part of the hiring process. The French Labour Code stipulates that the recruitment methods must be relevant to the pursued objective, that is, assessing the applicant's skills, and that the results must remain confidential. The job candidate must be able to obtain a copy of the test results.

2.3. EMPLOYMENT APPLICATIONS

Sections L. 5331-2 et seq. of the French Labour Code address the issue of job advertisements. For example, a job advertisement specifying a maximum age, or one drafted in a foreign language, may not be published. Job advertisements must not contain any false statements or information which could mislead applicants. Section L. 5321-2 of the French Labour Code also prohibits discrimination in job advertisements. Section L. 1142-1 of the French Labour Code provides that a job advertisement cannot specify the sex or marital status of the candidate sought, except where gender is a requirement for the position.

2.4. PRE-EMPLOYMENT TESTS AND EXAMINATIONS

It is prohibited in France to take into consideration health, disability and genetic characteristics as far as employment is concerned.

All employees must undergo a medical examination with a member of the occupational health service within three months from the employee's start date (or prior to this date for underage or night workers). By way of exception to this, employees assigned to a position that may present health or safety risks must undergo a more in-depth medical examination with an occupational health doctor that must take place before the employee's start date.

Systematic screening for drug or alcohol use is not lawful, but is authorized for safety-sensitive positions. Screening may be performed by the employer but must be mentioned in the employee handbook and the method used must be subject to control.[2]

The occupational health doctor can request that employees who will handle food or who are likely to sustain cuts in the course of their work undergo an AIDS test. The Charter of the Superior Council for the Prevention of Professional Risks (*Conseil supérieur de prévention des risques professionnels*) states that

---

2. See a recent example of this regarding drug screening: Administrative Supreme Court, 5 Dec. 2016, *no. 394178.*

no investigations may be carried out into whether an employee has AIDS, except in exceptional circumstances where there may be a direct link between this condition and the job offered.

2.5.   BACKGROUND, REFERENCE AND CREDIT CHECKS

Pre-hiring checks are quite rare in France. Future employers do sometimes verify a candidate's references and qualifications.

Data relating to offences, criminal convictions or security measures may only be collected under the control of an official authority. Many national collective bargaining agreements allow employers to ask job applicants to provide a police record disclosure (e.g., collective bargaining agreements for security companies, financial companies and private education institutions) or in the case of specific positions where a background check is justified by the responsibilities of the position (e.g., collective bargaining agreements for jewellers). Other collective bargaining agreements require that applicants sign an affidavit stating that they have never been convicted of a crime (that has not been pardoned or for which the applicant has not served the prison sentence or paid the fine) and are not involved in any current criminal legal proceedings or that they have not committed any criminal offences (collective bargaining agreements for security companies).

As a general rule, employers in France cannot ask questions about a candidate's credit or financial background, except in specific sectors (financial services, for example).

2.6.   INTERVIEWING

Pursuant to section L. 1221-6 of the French Labour Code, the information requested of the candidate in a job interview must be directly and necessarily related to the job offered, or to the assessment of the candidate's professional capabilities. The candidate must reply in good faith. Giving inaccurate information during a job interview can result in the employment contract being declared null and void if there was wilful misrepresentation (*dol*).

2.7.   HIRING PROCEDURES

The employer must fill out a pre-hiring declaration form for newly hired employees (*déclaration préalable à l'embauche*). The form must be sent to the local Social Security collection office (*URSSAF*) within eight days prior to the employee's start date. The single reporting form includes: registration of the employer with social security, registration of the employee with social security (unless on secondment), affiliation with an occupational medical centre, the organisation of the mandatory medical visit and affiliation with the State unemployment fund (*Pôle Emploi*).

In addition to the above-combined declaration, the following may also be required:

- When hiring his first employee, the employer must inform the labour inspector of the hiring.
- The employer has to register his company with the complementary pension funds within three months of setting up the business.
- When hiring a non-French employee (excluding European nationals), the necessary immigration formalities must be completed.
- The full names of all employees have to be recorded in the personnel ledger.
- The employer has to arrange for the employee to undergo a medical visit.

2.8. FINES AND PENALTIES

Gathering data on criminal convictions outside of the framework of legal provisions is a criminal offence pursuant to section 226-19 of the French Criminal Code.

Pursuant to section L. 1221-11 of the French Labour Code, non-compliance with the prior registration of the employee with the Social Security authorities can result in a fine equal to 300 times the minimum hourly wage. It may also constitute the criminal offence of illegal work.

2.9. CHECKLIST OF DOS AND DON'TS

- During job interviews, employers should avoid asking personal questions that are unrelated to the job that is being offered. For example, employers should not ask applicants if they have been treated by a psychologist or psychiatrist during the past ten years or if they are currently under a doctor's care, whether they practise safe sex, etc.

3. CONTRACTS OF EMPLOYMENT

3.1. OVERVIEW

An employment contract is defined as an agreement under which an individual undertakes to make their services available to another person, whether an individual or legal entity, and to place themselves under the management of that person in exchange for remuneration. An employment contract exists where the following three conditions are fulfilled:

- Performance of services.
- Remuneration.
- Legal subordination: It is the essential element to the definition of an employment contract, and is defined by the Court of Cassation as the *'performance of work under the authority of an employer who has the power to give orders and instructions, to supervise performance, and to sanction negligent behaviour on the part of the subordinate'*.[3]

If these three conditions are met, the contract qualifies as an employment relationship and the parties cannot exempt the employee from being covered by employment and social security legislation by giving the contract another name (e.g., independent contractor relationship).

Employment contracts can be for an indefinite-term or a fixed-term, and for full-time or part-time work.

3.2. Conclusion of the Employment Contract

3.2.1. Conditions of Validity

An employment contract is validly concluded provided, on the one hand, that it has a defined purpose and was concluded for a valid reason, that is, neither prohibited by law nor contrary to accepted standards of behaviour and public order, and, on the other hand, that the employer and the employee have the legal capacity to enter into the contract and gave their consent freely. In addition, the employer has to comply with the law related to the hiring of foreign workers (please refer to section 19.2).

Absent one of these conditions of validity, the employment contract can be ruled null by the judges.

An unlawful provision does not render the entire contract null, unless the provision was essential to the parties' consent.

For instance, the Court of Cassation has cancelled an employment contract where an employer had discovered that an employee had given inaccurate information about his prior work experience, considering that this information was decisive for the employer to hire the employee.

---

3. Employment Chamber of the Court of Cassation, 13 Nov. 1996, *no. 94-13.187.*

3.2.2. Written Employment Contract

Section L. 1221-2 of the French Labour Code states that an indefinite-term contract is *the normal and general form of the employment relationship.* A fixed-term employment contract is an exception which can only be entered into under specific conditions and must comply with particular regulations.

An employment contract does not have to be in writing (except for 'precarious' employment contracts and part-time employment contracts, as mentioned below), unless a collective bargaining agreement provides otherwise. In principle, an employment contract is formed as soon as the parties have agreed on the essential terms of the contract, which are the employee's duties, remuneration, place of work and working time arrangements.

Absent a written employment contract, the employee is presumed to have an indefinite-term contract.

Pursuant to section L. 1221-3 of the French Labour Code, when drafting a written employment contract the French language must be used. In addition, the French Labour Code provides that when the employee is not French, and the contract is a written contract, a translation of the contract into the foreign employee's language must be prepared if the employee so requests. In the event of a discrepancy between the foreign language and French version, only the contract in the foreign employee's language shall be binding against the employee. The contract must be drafted in two original copies, both of which must be signed and dated by the parties.

3.2.3. Offer Letters

Offer letters set out the basic terms upon which a position is offered by the employer and accepted by the prospective employee. The Court of Cassation has held on various occasions that a promise to hire, even if it is made orally, is binding on the employer provided that it is firm, that it is made to a particular person, and that it defines the job that is offered, the remuneration, the place of work and for the start date.[4]

Consequently, in the event the employer withdraws his offer letter, the employee is deemed to have been dismissed without a real and serious cause.[5]

An employee who accepts an offer letter and then goes back on their decision may be held civilly liable.

---

4. Employment Chamber of the Court of Cassation, 15 Dec. 2010, *no. 08-42.951.*
5. Employment Chamber of the Court of Cassation, 15 Dec. 2010, *no. 08-42.951.*

3.3. TERMS OF THE EMPLOYMENT CONTRACT

3.3.1. Specific Clauses

The parties who enter into an employment contract are free to determine the terms of the contract, provided that they comply with the conditions of validity described above (please refer to 3.2.1).

Certain clauses regarding duration or performance can be included in the contract provided that they are not prohibited by law.

Mobility clause: This is a provision under which the employer can change the employee's place of work within the geographical scope provided by the clause without the employee's consent. Such a clause is valid provided that the geographical scope of application is precisely defined.[6] With regard to the geographical scope, the Court of Cassation has ruled that a mobility clause allowing the employer to change the employee's place of work to anywhere in the whole of the French territory is valid and therefore enforceable.[7]

However, the Court of Cassation has ruled that, if the implementation of the mobility clause violates the right of the employee to a personal and family life, such violation must be proportionate and duly justified by the employer.[8]

Non-compete clause: Please refer to section 20.3.

Exclusivity clause: This a provision under which an employee commits to work for one employer on an exclusive basis.

Training commitment clause (clause de dédit-formation): This is a clause providing that an employee who resigns before a pre-determined period of time will have to reimburse the company the cost of the training. Nevertheless, in case of resignation, the employer cannot ask the employee to reimburse salaries which have been paid to him during the training period.[9]

Employment security clause (clause de garantie d'emploi): This is a clause under which the employer agrees not to terminate the contract during a certain period of time.

3.3.2. Trial Period

The trial period allows the employee to determine whether or not they like the position and allows the employer to assess the employee's ability to perform the job.

---

6. Employment Chamber of the Court of Cassation, 14 Oct. 2008, *no. 06-46.400.*
7. Employment Chamber of the Court of Cassation, 9 Jul. 2014, *no. 13-11.906.*
8. Employment Chamber of the Court of Cassation, 10 Feb. 2016, *no. 14-17.576.*
9. Employment Chamber of the Court of Cassation, 23 Oct. 2013, *no. 11-16.032.*

During the trial period, both employer and employee can terminate the contract without having to compensate the other, unless a collective bargaining agreement provides otherwise.

A trial period and the possibility of renewing it do not apply automatically. They must be expressly provided for in the offer letter or the employment contract.

Pursuant to the French Labour Code, the length of the trial period is as follows: two months for blue-collar workers and employees, three months for supervisors and technicians, and four months for executives.

If an employee is absent during the trial period, the trial period is extended for a duration equal to the absence, unless the absence is attributable to the employer.

The trial period can only be renewed once for a duration equal to the initial duration, provided that an extended industry-wide collective bargaining agreement, plus either the offer letter or the employment contract expressly provides for this possibility, and the employee gives his clear and unequivocal consent.[10,11]

The maximum durations of the trial period, including the renewal, are as follows: four months for blue-collar workers and employees, six months for supervisors and technicians, and eight months for executives.

An employer who wants to renew the trial period must inform the employee of this before the end of the initial trial period.[12]

At the end of the trial period, the employee is deemed to have been permanently hired if the employer did not terminate the contract.

A party who terminates the contract during the trial period does not have to justify their decision[13] or follow any particular procedure (except in the case of employee representatives). Nevertheless, there are some restrictions on the employer's right to terminate the contract during the trial period in certain cases (e.g., pregnant employees, employees who have sustained a work accident or who are suffering from a professional disease).

Where an employer terminates a contract containing a trial period of at least one week, the employer must give the employee twenty-four hours notice if the employee has worked for the company for less than eight days, forty-eight hours notice if the employee has worked for the company between eight days and one month, two weeks notice if the employee has worked for the company for more than one month, one month notice if the employee has worked

---

10. Employment Chamber of the Court of Cassation, 23 Jan. 1997, *no. 94-44.357.*
11. Employment Chamber of the Court of Cassation, 11 Oct. 2000, *no. 98-45.170.*
12. Employment Chamber of the Court of Cassation, 29 Nov. 2000, *no. 99-40.174.*
13. Employment Chamber of the Court of Cassation, 20 Oct. 2010, *no. 08-40.822.*

for the company for more than three months. The employment contract may provide for a longer notice period in case of termination by the employer.[14]

Termination of the trial period without prior notice will entitle the employee to compensatory payment equal to the wages they would have earned if they had worked until the end of the notice period.[15] The trial period, including renewal, cannot be extended because of the notice period.

When the employee terminates the contract during the trial period, they must give forty-eight hours notice. This is reduced to twenty-four hours if the employee has worked for the company for less than eight days.

3.4. MODIFICATION OF THE EMPLOYMENT CONTRACT

During the performance of the employment contract, the employer may wish to change the employee's working conditions.

A distinction must be made depending on whether this change results in a modification of a substantial element of the contract or whether it is simply a change in working conditions.

3.4.1. Modification of the Employment Contract Sensu Stricto

An employment contract typically sets out the employee's remuneration, duties, working time and place of work. These provisions form the contractual basis.

An employer cannot unilaterally impose a change to one or more elements of the employment contract (remuneration, working time, place of work, the employee's position) without the employee's consent.

3.4.2. Change in the Working Conditions

Where an employer decides to change employee's working conditions, such decision is binding on the employee. These types of decisions fall within the scope of the employer's managerial powers. If the employee refuses the change, he is deemed to have committed an act of misconduct. However, this is not necessarily, or in itself, an act of serious misconduct.[16,17,18]

---

14. Employment Chamber of the Court of Cassation, 15 Apr. 2016, *no. 15-12.588.*
15. Section L. 1221-25 of the French Labour Code.
16. Employment Chamber of the Court of Cassation, 10 Oct. 2000, *no. 98-41.358.*
17. Employment Chamber of the Court of Cassation, 27 Sep. 2006, *no. 04-47.005.*
18. Employment Chamber of the Court of Cassation, 23 Jan. 2008, *no. 07-40.522.*

3.4.3. The Procedure

When an employer wishes to make what qualifies as a substantial modification to an employee's employment contract for an economic reason, he informs the employee of the proposed new employment conditions and any accompanying measures by registered letter with acknowledgment of receipt.[19] The employer must also inform the employee that they have one month from receiving the letter to refuse the proposal. If the company is facing economic difficulties (receivership or liquidation proceedings), employees have fifteen days, instead of one month, from receipt of the letter to refuse the said proposal.[20] In the event that the employee does not refuse the proposal or does not answer within the relevant period, they are considered to have accepted the substantial modification of the employment contract.

This procedure does not need to be complied with if the modification is not based on economic reasons.[21] While the employer must inform the employee of the modification, there is no formal procedure to follow. Moreover, the employer must give the employee a sufficient amount of time to accept or refuse the proposed modification. In this respect, the French Labour Authorities suggest that employers give a fifteen-day period for reflection.

3.4.4. Consequences

If the employee accepts the modification of the employment contract, the new conditions will apply.

If the employee refuses the modification of the employment contract, the employer can either continue the contract under the initial conditions or dismiss the employee,[22] provided that the employer dismisses the employee for a reason other than the employee's refusal.

If, despite the employee's refusal to accept the modification of the employment contract, the employer imposes the modification, the employee can either ask the courts to rule that this is a case of unfair dismissal,[23] or formally declare that the employer terminated the contract[24] or ask for the judicial termination of the contract[25] which will result in an unfair dismissal or ask for the contract to be continued pursuant to the initial conditions.[26]

---

19. Employment Chamber of the Court of Cassation, 30 Jan. 2008, *no. 06-42.000.*
20. Section L. 1222-6 of the French Labour Code.
21. Employment Chamber of the Court of Cassation, 17 Nov. 2010, *no. 09-42.120.*
22. Employment Chamber of the Court of Cassation, 26 Nov. 2002, *no. 00-44.517.*
23. Employment Chamber of the Court of Cassation, 31 Mar. 2004, *no. 02-41.235.*
24. Employment Chamber of the Court of Cassation, 5 May 2010, *no. 07-45.409.*
25. Employment Chamber of the Court of Cassation, 6 Dec. 2011, *no. 10-19.918.*
26. Employment Chamber of the Court of Cassation, 26 Jun. 2001, *no. 99-42.489.*

3.5. CHECKLIST OF DOS AND DON'TS

– Avoid withdrawing an offer letter after it has been sent to the employee.
– Insert a trial period in the employment contract as well as the possibility of renewing it.
– When modifying the employment contract, employers must obtain the employee's consent. If the employer wishes to impose a change in the employee's working conditions, the employee's consent is not necessary.
– Provide the employee with a written employment contract in French at the time of hire, and, as the case may be, comply with the rules related to fixed-term contracts (as described in section 4) to avoid the contract being qualified as an indefinite-term contract.

4. 'PRECARIOUS' EMPLOYMENT CONTRACTS

4.1. OVERVIEW

The two most important types of 'precarious' employment contracts in France are fixed-term contracts (*contrats à durée déterminée*) and temporary employment contracts (*contrats de travail temporaire*).

The principle is that an indefinite-term contract should be used when entering into an employment relationship.

For the most part, temporary employment contracts are subject to the same rules as fixed-term contracts although they are subject to particular rules. Stringent rules have been put in place in order to limit the use of 'precarious' employment contracts.

4.2. FIXED-TERM EMPLOYMENT CONTRACTS

4.2.1. The Use of Fixed-Term Employment Contracts

A fixed-term employment contract or a temporary employment contract can only be entered into to perform a specific, temporary task. Moreover, pursuant to the French Labour Code, these contracts cannot be used on a long-term basis for jobs that are related to the company's ordinary business activities.

In addition, a fixed-term employment contract or temporary employment contract can be entered into in the following situations:

– Replacement of an employee who is temporarily absent from the company (e.g., an employee on paid leave, sick leave or maternity leave) or from their

position,[27] who has left the company and whose position will be removed, who has left the company or their position pending the hiring of a new employee under an indefinite-term contract.
- Temporary increase in business activity.
- Seasonal work.
- Customary fixed-term jobs to carry out work in those areas where it is common practice not to conclude indefinite-term contracts due to the type of work and its temporary nature (i.e., removals business, hotel work, teaching, professional sports, show business, etc.).

4.2.2. The Form and Content of a Fixed-Term Employment Contract

Pursuant to section L. 1242-12 of the French Labour Code, a fixed-term contract must be in writing and be given to the employee within two working days of being hired. If the contract is not in writing, it is deemed to be an indefinite-term contract.

In addition, it must contain the following clauses: the precise reason for using a fixed-term contract,[28] the name and professional functions of the replaced employee if the contract is concluded to replace an absent employee, the end date of the contract and, if applicable, the possibility to renew the contract if it has a precise end date, the minimum duration of the contract if it does not have a precise end date, a description of the job and position or the type of work that the employee performs at the company, the name of the collective bargaining agreement, the length of the trial period, if any, the amount of the remuneration and the structure thereof, if any, as well as the name and address of the supplementary pension fund and insurance institution.

4.2.3. End Date and Duration of the Contract

In principle, a fixed-term contract must stipulate the date on which it will expire. A fixed-term contract can be renewed twice at the most. However, the maximum duration of the contract, including the renewal, cannot exceed eighteen months; however, this maximum duration can be reduced to nine months or extended to twenty-four months in particular cases. In certain cases (to replace an absent employee or an employee who has left the company and who will be replaced by another employee hired under an indefinite-term contract, and in the case of seasonal work or customary fixed-term contracts),

---

27. Employment Chamber of the Court of Cassation, 4 Apr. 2012, *no. 10-20.007.*
28. Employment Chamber of the Court of Cassation, 5 Dec. 1989, *no. 86-44.316.*

it is possible not to stipulate a precise end date but only a minimum duration. However, it is not subject to a maximum duration.[29]

If no end date is stipulated, the contract terminates when the employee who was replaced returns to work or when the purpose of the contract has been achieved.

4.2.4. Conclusion of Successive Contracts

It is possible to enter into successive fixed-term employment contracts or successive temporary employment contracts, without interruption, with the same employee in order to replace an absent employee, or for seasonal work or customary fixed-term jobs. Apart from these three situations, it is not possible to conclude a new contract for the same job position unless a certain amount of time has elapsed, which depends on the term of the contract that has expired.

4.2.5. Termination of the Fixed-Term Contract

A fixed-term contract can be terminated before its end date only in the following situations: agreement between the parties, serious misconduct (*faute grave*), force majeure, in the event the occupational health doctor declares the employee unfit for work, hiring of the employee by another company under an indefinite-term contract.

Pursuant to the French Labour Code, at the end of the fixed-term contract, the contract stops automatically, regardless of whether a precise end date was stipulated.

In principle, at the end of the contract, the employee is entitled to a 'precarious' work indemnity equal to 10% of all the gross salary paid to the employee during the contract. Such indemnity shall not be payable if the contractual relationship is transformed into an indefinite-term contract, in particular in the event the fixed-term contract is reclassified as an indefinite-term contract.[30]

4.2.6. Fines and Penalties

A fixed-term contract is requalified as an indefinite-term contract in the following situations: conclusion of a fixed-term contract for a reason not permitted by law or to carry out a job corresponding to the company's normal and regular business activity or to replace an employee on strike or to carry

---

29. Employment Chamber of the Court of Cassation, 4 Feb. 2009, *no. 08-40.184.*
30. Employment Chamber of the Court of Cassation, 7 Jul. 2015, *no. 13-17.195.*

out dangerous work, absence of written contract, absence of an essential clause in the contract, violation of the rules regarding the end date, duration and renewal of the contract, non-compliance with the waiting period between two successive contracts for the same job, continuation of the contractual relationship after expiry of the contract.

In the event that a fixed-term contract is requalified as an indefinite-term contract, the employee is entitled to compensation at least equal to one month's salary. In addition, if the employer wishes to terminate the contract, he must comply with the dismissal procedure.

Failure to comply with the rules related to fixed-term contracts can result in a fine of (EUR) 3,750, and in the event of a repeated offence, a six-month prison term and a fine of EUR 7,500.

If the employer terminates the contract before its end, the damages are at least equal to the wages that should have been paid to the employee until the end of the contract, plus the 'precarious' work indemnity if applicable, and compensation for accrued leave not yet taken. If the employee terminates the contract for reasons other than the above, such employee may be liable to pay the employer damages depending on the harm suffered, which will be assessed at the judge's discretion.

4.3. TEMPORARY WORK

The temporary work relationship consists of three parties: the temporary employment agency, the company using the worker's services and the worker, which means that three relationships need to be examined.

4.3.1. Relationship between the Temporary Employment Agency and the User Company

When a temporary employment agency places an employee on assignment with the user company, the two enter into a written contract for the supply of temporary staff (*contrat de mise à disposition*).

Pursuant to sections L. 1251-5 et seq. of the French Labour Code, the contract must also comply with the following requirements:

– The contract must be in writing and be signed within two working days following the date on which the temporary worker begins working for the user company.
– The contract must state why a temporary worker is being used; these reasons are the same as for fixed-term contracts (please refer to section 4.2.1).

– The contract must stipulate the end date of the assignment and, if applicable, that there is the possibility of modifying this end date.
– The contract must describe the position, the skills and experience required, the place where the assignment is to be carried out and the working hours.
– The contract must state the type of protective equipment that the employee will use, if any.
– The contract must stipulate the amount of the remuneration and the structure thereof.

In addition and pursuant to section R. 4161-5 of the French Labour Code, the user company must inform the temporary employment agency on a yearly basis of the professional risk factors encountered by the temporary worker in the context of their position held within the user company. The purpose of this information is to draw up an individual risk prevention record (*'fiche individuelle de prévention'*).

4.3.2. Relationship between the Temporary Employment Agency and the Temporary Worker

A temporary employment agency hires workers for the purpose of placing them on assignment at another company for a specific period of time. This contract is called a temporary employment contract (*contrat de mission*). Its main characteristics are as follows:

– It is for a fixed term.
– It must be in writing.
– It must reiterate the clauses and information set out in the contract for the supply of temporary staff.
– It must also set out notably the employee's position, a breakdown of the components of the remuneration including the 'precarious' work indemnity, the trial period if any, and a statement that the user company is allowed to hire the employee upon completion of the assignment.
– If the temporary employment agency terminates the temporary employment contract before the agreed term, in the absence of a force majeure event or serious misconduct on the part of the employee, it must offer the employee a new contract within three days without any substantial changes to the employee's position, remuneration, working hours and travel time, or pay the employee his remuneration until the agreed term, including the 'precarious' work indemnity.

The contract must be remitted to the employee at the latest within two working days of the day the employee is made available.

Temporary workers must be equally treated with regard to permanent staff.

It should be noted that, as from 19 August 2015, temporary employment agencies may enter into 'indefinite-term temporary employment contracts' with workers. This legal framework will be in force until 31 December 2018 and will be the subject of a governmental report due 30 June 2018 on its conditions of application and the possibility of introducing it permanently.

4.3.3. Relationship between the User Company and the Temporary Worker

While there is no contract between the user company and the temporary worker, the user company is granted authority over the temporary worker pursuant to the contract for the supply of temporary staff. It can give instructions to the temporary worker, and is vicariously liable for the worker's actions.

The user company is also responsible for the conditions under which the work is performed in accordance with applicable laws, regulations and collective bargaining agreements. In particular, the user company is responsible for the health and safety of temporary employees. It also has the same obligations vis-à-vis temporary workers and permanent employees concerning collective work areas, the company cafeteria, etc.

If the user company continues to give work to a temporary worker after expiry of the assignment but does not sign a new contract for the supply of temporary staff, the worker is deemed to have an indefinite-term employment contract with the user company and is credited with length of service from the first day of his original assignment.

4.3.4. Fines and Penalties

Civil Liability

If the legal requirements are not complied with, the employee can claim to benefit from an indefinite-term contact either with the user company or with the temporary work agency, and damages.

Criminal Liability

The user company and the temporary work agency can be ordered to pay a fine of EUR 3,750 and, in case of repeated offences, be sentenced to a six-month prison term and a fine of EUR 7,500.

4.4. CHECKLIST OF DOS AND DON'TS

– Comply with the rules related to 'precarious' employment contracts in order to avoid the contract being requalified as an indefinite-term contract.

5. MANAGING PERFORMANCE/CONDUCT

5.1. OVERVIEW

Employee management enables employers to obtain optimum productivity and performance from employees. In this respect, there are various methods of assessing employee performance, which are used with increasing frequency in France.

5.2. WRITTEN EVALUATIONS

Employee evaluations can take various forms:

– Annual assessment interview.
– Career development interview.
– Ranking by quotas: It is used in certain international groups and consists of ranking employees in different categories depending on performance. Under this system, a certain number of employees must be ranked in each category, without regard to skills or objective criteria.
– The Court of Cassation ruled that this type of assessment method is not legal.[31] This decision means that only the employees' skills can be taken into account during the assessment, and these skills cannot be under or overestimated in order to comply with the pre-determined quotas.

5.3. CHECKLIST OF DOS AND DON'TS

– During the annual assessment, the employee should be encouraged to discuss any performance issues with their superior.

---

31. Employment Chamber of the Court of Cassation 27 Mar. 2013, *no. 11-26.539.*

6. DISCIPLINARY POWER OF THE EMPLOYER

6.1. OVERVIEW

An employer has the authority to give the employee instructions and punish any violations.

In this respect, employers have a wide range of sanctions at their disposal which allow them to take the most appropriate sanction in light of the employee's behaviour.

6.2. EMPLOYEE HANDBOOKS

Pursuant to section L. 1311-2 of the French Labour Code, employee handbooks or company rules and regulations (for the remainder of this section, the term 'company rules and regulations' will be used) must be drawn up by companies or establishments regularly employing twenty or more employees. The company rules and regulations must be drafted in French.

6.2.1. Content of Employee Handbooks/Company Rules and Regulations

The content of company rules and regulations is exhaustively defined in section L. 1321-1 of the French Labour Code, which stipulates that they must set out the:

> 'measures for application of health and safety regulations in the company or establishment [...]; the conditions in which the employees can be asked to participate, at the employer's request, in restoring working conditions which protect the health and safety of the employees, as soon as working conditions appear compromised; and, the general and permanent rules relating to discipline, particularly the nature and scope of the disciplinary sanctions that the employer can take'.

Moreover, the company rules and regulations may include provisions promoting the principle of neutrality within the company and limiting the extent to which employees can manifest their convictions. However, such restrictions are only valid if they are justified by the exercise of other fundamental rights and freedoms or if they are necessary for the proper running of the company and they are proportionate to the pursued objective.[32]

Clauses relating to matters not provided for by the law are null and void.

---

32. Section L. 1321-2-1 of the French Labour Code.

Section L. 1321-3 of the French Labour Code prohibits:

> 'provisions which are contrary to applicable laws and regulations and to the stipulations of collective bargaining agreements that are applicable in the company or establishment; provisions introducing restrictions on employees' rights and on individual and collective freedoms, which are not justified by the nature of the task to be carried out or are not proportionate to the pursued objective; as well as provisions which discriminate against employees in their employment or their work, with equal professional capacities, due to their origin, their sex, their customs, their sexual orientation or gender identity, their age, their family situation or pregnancy, their genetic characteristics, their belonging or not, whether actually or supposedly, to an ethnic group, a nation or a race, their political opinions, their activities in trade unions or mutual organizations, their religious convictions, their physical appearance, their surname or due to their health or a handicap'.

6.2.2. Implementing and Amending Employee Company Rules and Regulations

Company rules and regulations and any subsequent amendments can only be adopted once they have been submitted to the works council for opinion, or, as the case may be, to the employee representatives and to the health and safety committee (*comité d'hygiène, de sécurité et des conditions de travail* or *CHSCT*) if any. Failure to do so can result in criminal sanctions and deprive the rules and regulations or subsequent amendments of their effects.[33]

The employer is also required to send two copies of the company rules and regulations to the labour inspector before implementing them. The labour inspector can at any time order the deletion or amendment of any provisions which are contrary to the law.

6.3. DISCIPLINARY SANCTIONS

As mentioned above, the law does not set out a list of sanctions. The company rules and regulations define types of inappropriate conduct and set out the nature and scale of the sanctions that can be taken by the employer.

An oral reprimand cannot be considered as a sanction.[34] However, criticisms or warnings sent to an employee in writing constitute a sanction.

---

33. Employment Chamber of the Court of Cassation, 11 Feb. 2015, *no. 13-16.457.*
34. Circular of 15 Mar. 1983.

In addition, transferring an employee because of their conduct is a sanction.

Disciplinary sanctions other than dismissal may be taken against an employee only if such disciplinary sanctions are provided for in the company rules and regulations.[35]

An employer can also suspend an employee's contract (*mise à pied*). In this respect, there are two types of suspension in the context of disciplinary action. A suspension is deemed to be a sanction if its purpose is to punish inappropriate behaviour. In this case, it is a disciplinary suspension (*mise à pied disciplinaire*). If the purpose of the suspension is to give the employer time to consider what type of disciplinary action to take against the employee, then it is a precautionary suspension (*mise à pied conservatoire*). This is a precautionary measure when the employer considers that the employee's conduct is such that it warrants their immediate removal from the company.

In addition, fines and other pecuniary sanctions are strictly prohibited under French law. Any provisions to the contrary are deemed null and void and may give rise to criminal sanctions.

An employee cannot be disciplined twice for the same act of misconduct. In a case in which an employee received a warning and was then dismissed, without this dismissal being based on new facts, the dismissal was held to be unfair.[36]

6.4. DISCIPLINARY PROCEDURE

Prior to informing an employee that disciplinary action will be taken, the employer must invite the employee to a preliminary meeting. When initiating this procedure, the employer can choose to suspend the employee as a precautionary measure if the misconduct requires such action.

All sanctions, except a warning or a sanction similar to a warning which does not impact, immediately or subsequently, the employee's presence in the company, or their position, career or remuneration, require that a preliminary meeting be held with the employee.

In principle, the employer is allowed to choose the type of disciplinary action that he believes is most appropriate in light of the employee's conduct. Nevertheless, the sanction must be proportionate to the fault that was committed.

The employer must wait at least two working days after the preliminary meeting has taken place before informing the employee of the disciplinary action that will be taken. Such notification must be set out in a letter delivered to the employee by hand or by registered letter with acknowledgment of receipt and must be sent within one month of the preliminary meeting.

---

35. Employment Chamber of the Court of Cassation, 23 Mar. 2017, *no. 15-23.090.*
36. Employment Chamber of the Court of Cassation, 13 Nov. 2001, *no. 99-42.709.*

Disciplinary action must be taken within two months from the date on which the employer becomes aware of the misconduct.

In addition, the employer can sanction an employee who continues in his wrongful behaviour after the notification of the first sanction, even if he has not yet received this notification.[37]

6.5. CONTROL OF THE JUDGE

An employee can challenge a disciplinary measure in court. In such case, the court will assess whether the process was validly carried out and whether the alleged facts justify the disciplinary action.

Unless the sanction is a dismissal or the termination of a fixed-term contract for serious misconduct, the courts can cancel a sanction that is irregular as to form, or that is unfair or disproportionate.

6.6. CHECKLIST OF DOS AND DON'TS

– Comply with the disciplinary procedure in order to avoid the sanction being cancelled.
– Act quickly in order to avoid the conduct becoming time-barred (within two months from the date on which the employer becomes aware of the facts).
– Do not impose financial penalties on employees.
– Employees cannot be disciplined twice for the same misconduct.

7. MUTUAL TERMINATION AGREEMENT

7.1. OVERVIEW

Indefinite-term employment contracts may be terminated by mutual agreement between the employer and the employee by means of a mutual termination agreement (*rupture conventionnelle*). Even before the mutual termination agreement was specifically provided for in the French Labour Code, the Court of Cassation had acknowledged the possibility, based on section 1193 of the French Civil Code, for employers and employees to terminate their employment contract by mutual consent. With the mutual termination agreement being specifically provided for in sections L. 1237-11 et seq. of the French Labour Code since 2008, the question arose as to whether employers and employees

---

37. Employment Chamber of the Court of Cassation, 12 Feb. 2013, *no. 12-15.330.*

could still negotiate a mutual termination outside of the legal framework of sections L. 1237-11 et seq.

In a widely commented decision of 15 October 2014,[38] the Court of Cassation answered in the negative: unless otherwise provided by law, the mutual termination of the employment contract can only be implemented in compliance and according to the provisions of L. 1237-11, i.e., exclusively within the legal framework of a mutual termination agreement *(rupture conventionnelle).*

It should also be noted that mutual termination agreements can be entered into on economic grounds within the context of a workforce reduction.

7.2.   THE PROCEDURE

A mutual termination agreement can be signed between the employee and the employer if they both wish to terminate the employment relationship. In this regard, it was necessary to determine whether such an agreement could be signed at any time during the employment contract and notably whether such agreement could be signed, for example, while the employment contract was suspended. On 30 September 2014,[39] the Court of Cassation held that such a mutual termination agreement can be entered into while the employment contract is suspended further to an occupational accident or occupational disease as well as during maternity leave.[40]

In addition, if they are involved in a particular dispute, such dispute will not have an impact on the validity of the mutual termination agreement. However, a party cannot oblige the other to accept the mutual termination agreement.[41]

Certain conditions must be fulfilled in order for a mutual termination agreement to be valid:

– The parties must have been free to agree to the principle of termination and to its terms and conditions (date of termination, the amount of the specific termination compensation which cannot be less than the amount of the severance pay due by law or under the collective bargaining agreement, etc.).
– One or several meetings must be held between the employer and the employee who can both be assisted. If no meeting has been held, the mutual termination agreement is considered to be null and void, but it is up to the employee to prove no meetings were held.[42]
– A written agreement must be executed setting out the date and the terms and conditions of the termination. In fact, the parties complete and sign

38.   Employment Chamber of the Court of Cassation, 15 Oct. 2014, *no. 11-22.251.*
39.   Employment Chamber of the Court of Cassation, 30 Sep. 2014, *no. 13-16.297.*
40.   Employment Chamber of the Court of Cassation, 25 Mar. 2015, *no. 14-10.149.*
41.   Employment Chamber of the Court of Cassation, 23 May 2013, *no. 12-13.865.*
42.   Employment Chamber of the Court of Cassation, 1 Dec. 2016, no. 15-21.609.

a standard request form which will subsequently be sent to the Labour Authorities (the so-called *DIRECCTE*). A copy of this standard request form must be provided to the employee. If not, the mutual termination agreement is considered to be null and void.[43] With regard to the date of termination of the employment contract, the Court of Cassation has recently ruled that the date set out in the mutual termination agreement, if fixed subsequently to the Labour Authority's approval, is legally binding for the employment tribunal. As a consequence, the employment tribunal cannot order the employer to deliver a new work certificate and statement of the French employment office *(Pôle Emploi)*, mentioning, as date of termination, the date of the Labour Authority's approval rather than the date provided for in the mutual termination agreement.[44]

– Either party can revoke the agreement within fifteen calendar days of signing the request form by informing the other party by any means.[45]
– Upon expiry of the fifteen-day consideration period (assuming neither party has revoked the agreement), the request form must be sent to the Labour Authorities. If such request is sent before expiry of the consideration period, it will automatically be rejected.[46]
– The Labour Authorities have fifteen working days to approve the mutual termination agreement. If no answer is given within this period, the agreement is deemed to be approved, even if a refusal decision is received by the parties shortly after expiry of this period.[47]
– The earliest the termination can take effect is the day after the approval has been given.

During the fifteen-day approval period, the Labour Authorities verify that the statutory conditions relating to the termination procedure have been complied with and that the parties freely consented to the agreement.

The validity of a mutual termination agreement can be challenged within a period of twelve months from the approval of the agreement.

As a mutual termination agreement is not like a settlement agreement, under which the employee waives his right to bring future claims, the employee can still file claims in connection with the performance of their employment contract (such as requests for back pay) (refer to section 30.3.4). In this respect, the Court of Cassation held, in a decision issued in late 2014, that employees, in the event they had not received the minimum amount of the specific termination compensation, are entitled to turn to the Courts in order to claim additional compensation.[48]

---

43. Employment Chamber of the Court of Cassation, 6 Feb. 2013, *no. 11-27.000.*
44. Employment Chamber of the Court of Cassation, 18 Feb. 2015, *no. 13-23.880.*
45. Employment Chamber of the Court of Cassation, 6 Oct. 2015, *no. 14-17.539.*
46. Employment Chamber of the Court of Cassation, 14 Jan. 2016, *no. 14-26.220.*
47. Employment Chamber of the Court of Cassation, 16 Dec. 2015, *no. 13-27.212.*
48. Employment Chamber of the Court of Cassation, 10 Dec. 2014, *no. 13-22.134.*

When mutual termination agreements are concluded within the context of a workforce reduction, they must be taken into account to establish the employer's obligations regarding collective redundancy procedures (see in particular sections 9.1 et seq.) if the following conditions are met:

(1)   such termination agreements have an economic cause;
(2)   they are part of a workforce reduction process;
(3)   they have been approved by the Labour Authorities.

7.3.   CHECKLIST OF DOS AND DON'TS

–   Do not set out in the mutual termination agreement a termination date which is prior to the expiry of the fifteen-day period during which the Labour Authorities can approve or reject the mutual termination agreement.

8.   TERMINATION OF AN EMPLOYMENT CONTRACT FOR PERSONAL REASONS

8.1.   OVERVIEW

In France, employees' employment contracts can be terminated either for 'personal' reasons (e.g., because of their conduct) or for economic reasons. If the 'personal' reasons for termination constitute serious or wilful misconduct, the employee is not entitled to any severance compensation (except compensation for paid leave not taken).

8.2.   GROUNDS FOR DISMISSING AN EMPLOYEE FOR 'PERSONAL' REASONS

A dismissal for 'personal' reasons must be based on a 'real and serious' cause.

An employer can dismiss an employee for misconduct (*faute simple*). A misconduct justifies termination of the employment contract, but is not of sufficient gravity to justify immediate termination without notice (unlike serious or wilful misconduct (*faute grave ou lourde*), which is defined in section 8.4). Under French labour law, other situations can constitute a 'real and serious' cause for dismissal even if they do not qualify as serious For example, long or repeated absences due to sickness, physical incapacity subsequent to an illness or an accident and the inability to reassign the employee elsewhere in the company, professional insufficiency and the inability to meet assigned targets.

8.3.   Dismissal Procedure

If an employer intends to dismiss an employee for 'personal' reasons, he must first ask the employee to attend a pre-dismissal meeting (section L. 1232-2 of the French Labour Code).

The employer must wait five working days (Saturdays included) after the first attempt has been made to deliver the registered or hand-delivered letter to the employee before holding the pre-dismissal meeting.

Pursuant to section L. 1232-3 of the French Labour Code, during the pre-dismissal meeting, the employer or his representative must inform the employee of the reason(s) why the company is considering terminating their employment contract, and listen to the employee's explanations.

If the employer still wishes to dismiss the employee after the pre-dismissal meeting, the employer cannot give the employee notice of termination until at least two working days (Saturdays included) after the pre-dismissal meeting.

8.4.   Fines and Penalties

An employee who is dismissed is entitled to:

– Compensation for paid leave not taken.
– Compensation in lieu of notice.
– Severance pay which is provided by the law, the collective bargaining agreement or, in some cases, the employment contract.
– Damages for unfair dismissal whose amount varies depending on the total number of employees at the company and the employee's length of service.
– Damages in case of irregular dismissal: if the employer did not follow the pre-dismissal meeting procedure or if the employer gave the employee notice of their dismissal without complying with the prescribed time limits. The amount of these damages will depend on the total number of employees at the company and the employee's length of service.
– If the employment contract has been terminated because of the employee's serious misconduct (*faute grave*), the employee will not be entitled to severance pay, nor compensation in lieu of notice. Serious misconduct is misconduct of such gravity that it requires terminating immediately the employment contract without notice. If the employment contract has been terminated because of the employee's wilful misconduct (*faute lourde*), the employee will not be entitled to severance pay nor compensation in lieu of notice. Wilful misconduct shows the employee's intent to harm the employer and allows the latter to bring an action for damages against the employee.

The courts can rule that a dismissal is null and void only if this is possible under the French Labour Code or if the employer violated a fundamental freedom,[49] for example, if the employee was dismissed for a discriminatory reason or if the employee reported, in good faith, facts that could be qualified as criminal offences.[50]

If the dismissal is held to be null and void, the employee is entitled to be reinstated in their position or an equivalent one,[51] unless such reinstatement is physically impossible. In addition, the reinstated employee is entitled to the remuneration they should have received from the time of the dismissal until reinstatement.[52]

If it is physically impossible to reinstate the employee or if the employee does not ask to be reinstated, they will be entitled to compensation in lieu of notice, severance pay and damages equal to six months' salary regardless of the employee's length of service and the size of the company.

8.5. Checklist of Dos and Don'ts

– Do not dismiss an employee for a discriminatory reason.

9. LAYOFFS, REDUCTIONS IN WORKFORCE AND/OR REDUNDANCIES AS A RESULT OF JOB ELIMINATIONS OR OTHER RESTRUCTURING

9.1. Overview

Section L. 1233-3 of the French Labour Code defines a redundancy as:

A 'dismissal by the employer on one or more grounds unrelated to the employee personally, resulting from the elimination or transformation of the employee's position, or an amendment, refused by the employee, of an essential component of the employment contract', following, *inter alia*:

– economic difficulties, examples of which are given by the French Labour Code;
– technological changes;
– reorganization to safeguard competitiveness;
– cessation of activity of the company.

A redundancy must be justified by a real and serious cause.

---

49. Employment Chamber of the Court of Cassation, 31 Mar. 2004, *no. 01-46.960.*
50. Employment Chamber of the Court of Cassation, 30 Jun. 2016, *no. 15-10.557.*
51. Employment Chamber of the Court of Cassation, 30 Mar. 2003, *no. 00-44.811.*
52. Employment Chamber of the Court of Cassation, 25 Jan. 2006, *no. 03-47.517.*

The French Labour Code strictly regulates redundancies. If a dismissal meets the definition of redundancy, the employer has to comply with a number of obligations, including consulting the employee representative bodies, preparing a job protection plan (*plan de sauvegarde de l'emploi*) as the case may be, informing the Labour Authorities and allowing the employee to take an outplacement leave (*congé de reclassement*) or take part in a professional protection scheme (*contrat de sécurisation professionnelle*), etc.

There are three types of redundancies: individual redundancies, collective redundancies of less than ten employees and collective redundancies of at least ten employees within a period of thirty consecutive days. The company's obligations depend on the number of redundancies, added of the number of other terminations for economic reasons (such as voluntary departures by mutually agreed termination).

9.2. JUSTIFICATION OF A REDUNDANCY

The definition of a redundancy contains three cumulative conditions:

– *Grounds unrelated to the employee personally*: The grounds for the dismissal must be unrelated to the employee personally;
– *Material justification*: An employer can make employees redundant if the economic reason (see below) results in the elimination or transformation of a job or an amendment to the employment contract that the employee refused;
– *Economic justification*: Pursuant to the French Labour law, the elimination or transformation of a job, or an amendment to the employment contract, must result from, notably: economic difficulties, technological changes, reorganization to safeguard competitiveness, cessation of activity of the company. The 2016 labour law reform defines economic difficulties as a significant change in at least one economic indicator, such as a decline in orders or turnover, operating losses, a deterioration of the cash flow situation, a fall in gross operating profit, or any other element which could justify these difficulties. A decline in orders or turnover is assessed differently depending on the number of employees of the undertaking. A decline in orders or turnover is deemed to be significant when, compared to the same period in the preceding year, it continues for a period of at least:
– one-quarter, in an undertaking with less than 11 employees;
– two-quarters, in an undertaking with between 11 and 50 employees;
– three-quarters, in an undertaking with between 50 and 300 employees;
– four-quarters, in an undertaking with 300 or more employees.

9.3. REDEPLOYMENT OBLIGATION

As soon as an employer contemplates making an employee redundant, the employer must make every effort during the entire process to try to redeploy the employee within the 'establishments' or other group companies.

The redeployment offers must be made before and until such time as the employee is notified of their redundancy. Failure to comply with this obligation will render the redundancy unfair even if the company has valid economic justification.

9.4. PROCEDURES OF REDUCTIONS IN WORKFORCE/REDUNDANCIES/ JOB ELIMINATIONS

9.4.1. Selection Criteria

As soon as the decision to make one or more employees redundant is taken, the employer must establish the selection criteria that will be used to determine which employees will be made redundant. In this respect, the employer must apply the criteria set out in the collective bargaining agreement applicable within the company. If the collective bargaining agreement does not set out such criteria, the employer must apply all of the selection criteria set out in the French Labour Code. These include the number of dependents, length of service in the establishment or the company, particular circumstances that would make it difficult for the employee to find new employment (such as a disability or the employee's age) and professional skills (section L. 1233-5 of the French Labour Code).

The employer can favour one of these criteria provided, however, he takes into account all the other criteria provided under the French Labour Code.

If an employer fails to comply with the selection criteria rules, they may be held criminally liable and ordered to pay a fine of EUR 750 (for a private individual) or EUR 3,750 (for a legal entity). However, the courts will not rule that the redundancies are unfair,[53] but the employees will be entitled to damages in order to compensate the harm resulting from the unjustified loss of their job.[54]

---

53. Employment Chamber of the Court of Cassation, 5 Dec. 2006, *no. 04-48.800.*
54. Employment Chamber of the Court of Cassation, 23 Nov. 2011, *no. 10-30.768.*

9.4.2.   Individual Redundancies

Pre-dismissal Meeting

Before making an employee redundant, the employer must call the employee to a pre-dismissal meeting. The procedure is the same as for a dismissal for 'personal' reasons (for more details please refer to section 8.3).

The purpose of this meeting is to discuss the company's economic situation and explain to the employee how it will impact their job.

During the meeting, the employer must offer the employee the possibility to take part in a professional security scheme (*contrat de sécurisation professionnelle*) if the company or the group to which it belongs employs fewer than 1,000 employees, or give them information about the outplacement leave (*congé de reclassement*) if the company or the group to which it belongs employs more than 1,000 employees.

Notification of the redundancy

If it is not possible to redeploy the employee, the employer will be able to give the employee notice of their redundancy. Once the pre-dismissal meeting has been held, the employer must wait seven working days (fifteen days for executives) before being able to give the employee notice of their redundancy.

Informing the Labour authorities

The employer must inform the Labour Authorities (*DIRECCTE*) of the redundancy within eight days thereof.

9.4.3.   Redundancies of Fewer than Ten Employees over a Thirty-Day Period

When an employer contemplates making at least two but fewer than ten employees redundant over a thirty-day period, the employer must inform and consult the works council, if any, or the staff delegates on the proposed collective redundancies and the proposed restructuring.

If the employer fails to do so, he may be held criminally liable.

After informing and consulting the employee representatives, the employer must ask the employees to attend a pre-dismissal meeting. For more details about this procedure, refer to section 8.3.

9.4.4. Redundancies of at Least Ten Employees over a Thirty-Day Period in Companies that Employ at Least Fifty Employees

When an employer contemplates making at least ten employees redundant over a thirty-day period in a company with at least fifty employees, the employer must inform and consult the works council on the proposal and implement a job protection plan (*plan de sauvegarde de l'emploi*) containing a redeployment plan.

According to sections L. 1233-24-1 and L. 1233-24-4 of the French Labour Code, the redundancy procedure and the provisions of the job protection plan are determined either by a majority agreement concluded between the employer and the employee representative trade unions or by a document drafted by the employer (the 'unilateral document').

The employer and the employee representative trade unions have the option of concluding a collective bargaining agreement *which must set out the provisions of the job protection plan* and which may also (although it is not an obligation) establish the conditions under which the works council will be consulted on the collective redundancies and how such redundancies will be implemented (section L. 1233-24-1 of the French Labour Code).

The employer is not under any obligation to hold such negotiations with the representative trade unions in order to conclude a collective bargaining agreement. The employer can unilaterally draft a document detailing how the dismissals will be carried out, but this will involve stricter control by the Labour Authorities (*DIRECCTE*).

In both cases, the documents must be approved by the Labour Authorities, which can, during the process, submit observations or propose amendments with respect to the process or measures contained in the job protection plan.

The Labour Authorities' control depends on whether a majority collective bargaining agreement has been concluded with representative trade unions or whether a unilateral document has been drawn up by the employer.

The Labour Authorities must give the company notice of their decision within a period of fifteen days from receipt of the collective bargaining agreement or within twenty-one days from receipt of the unilateral document.

Once the Labour Authorities have approved the collective agreement or the unilateral document, the employer can give the employees notice of their redundancy, while respecting a period of thirty days between the Labour Authorities being notified of the collective bargaining agreement or unilateral document and notifying the employees of redundancy.

9.4.5. Redundancies of At Least Ten Employees over a Thirty-Day Period in Companies with Fewer than Fifty Employees

An employer employing fewer than fifty employees and who contemplates making at least ten employees redundant must consult the staff delegates after sending them certain information.

At the same time, the employer must also send the same information to the Labour Authorities and a separate document setting out the measures of the redundancy plan. The Labour Authorities will then verify whether the employer complied with the staff representative consultation procedure.

After having informed the Labour Authorities of the proposed redundancies, the employer must wait thirty days before giving the employees notice of their redundancy.

9.5. FINES AND PENALTIES

Where at least ten employees are made redundant over a thirty-day period in companies with at least fifty employees, the employees can challenge the validity of their dismissal in court on the grounds that the employer did not set up a job protection plan, or that the plan set up was inadequate, in order to have their redundancy declared null and void.

Any redundancies that are notified before the Labour Authorities have approved the collective agreement or the unilateral document (or before the end of the approval period), are null and void.

9.6. EMPLOYMENT SAFEGUARD AGREEMENT

Under section L. 5125-1 of the French Labour Code, if a company is facing serious economic difficulties, a company-wide collective bargaining agreement can be concluded between the employer and the employee representative trade unions in order to make adjustments to the employees' working time and remuneration. Such agreement can provide that the employees' gross remuneration and/or working hours will be reduced for a set period of time that may not exceed five years and in return, the company undertakes not to reduce the workforce for a period of time at least equal to the term of the company-wide collective bargaining agreement.

The agreement must set out or, failing this, the employer must inform all the employees concerned of the conditions under which they have the right to accept or refuse to have the agreement apply to their employment contract.

The employees have one month to refuse application of the agreement to their employment contract. If the employees fail to make known their refusal within this one-month period, they will be deemed to have accepted.

If the employee accepts that the agreement be applied to him, the implementation of this agreement suspends any provisions of the employment contract that are contrary to the agreement. If the employee does not give his consent, their employment contract will be terminated for individual economic reason. However, in such cases, the employer will not have any duty to accommodate, any training obligation or any redeployment obligation toward this employee.

The agreement also contains a penalty clause under which the employees are entitled to damages if the employer fails to comply with his obligations, in particular that of not dismissing any employees.

9.7. AGREEMENTS TO SAVE JOBS OR CREATE EMPLOYMENT

In addition to employment safeguard agreements, also called 'defensive agreements' (please refer to section 9.6), the 2016 labour law reform enables employers to enter into a new kind of collective bargaining agreement: 'proactive agreements'.

Under section L. 2254-2 of the French Labour Code, a company-wide collective bargaining agreement may be negotiated with the company's union delegates to save jobs or create employment. Provisions of this new kind of agreement automatically replace any contrary provisions in employees' employment contracts, including in terms of remuneration and working time. However, a reduction in employees' monthly remuneration is excluded.

If the employee refuses that the agreement be applied to him, the employer may dismiss the employee on this specific ground – different from a dismissal for personal reasons or for economic reasons – which cannot be challenged in court. In this case, such dismissal is subject to the procedure applicable to individual redundancies.

9.8. CHECKLIST OF DOS AND DON'TS

- Set up a job protection plan if at least ten employees will be made redundant over a thirty-day period if the company has fifty employees or more.
- Make every effort to try to redeploy the employees. Determine whether any positions are available within the company or the group, and offer those positions to the employees whose redundancy is being considered.
- Consult the works council in order to avoid any criminal liability.

10. TRANSFERS OF UNDERTAKINGS

10.1. OVERVIEW

French employment law strictly regulates acquisitions and disposals of businesses. In particular, the French Labour Code provides for the automatic transfer of the employment contracts in the event of an asset sale where there is a transfer of an 'autonomous economic entity'.

10.2. CONDITIONS OF TRANSFER OF EMPLOYMENT CONTRACTS

Section L. 1224-1 of the French Labour Code stipulates that:

When there is a change in the legal situation of the employer, particularly through succession, sale, merger, transformation of the business or conversion of the undertaking into a company, all the employment contracts in force on the day of the change shall continue between the new employer and the undertaking's employees.

The article targets any *change in the legal situation of the employer*. The term is broad and covers situations as diverse as successions, sales and even mergers.

The Court of Cassation considers that section L. 1224-1 of the French Labour Code applies if the transaction relates to an autonomous economic entity, that is, an organized grouping of personnel and tangible/intangible assets allowing the exercise of an economic activity pursuing its own specific objective and retaining its identity.

10.3. CONSEQUENCES OF THE TRANSFER OF AN UNDERTAKING

10.3.1. Consequences on the Employees

If the conditions of section L. 1224-1 of the French Labour Code are met, the employment contracts concluded with the seller company are automatically transferred to the transferee.

Under no circumstances can the transferor and the transferee by mutual agreement oppose the transfer of the employment contracts in force. The employees cannot refuse their transfer either.

All of the terms of the transferred employment contracts continue to apply under the same conditions, and calculation of the length of service with the transferor will continue with the new employer.

10.3.2.   Consequences on Collective Benefits

Please refer to 13.6.

10.4.   FINES AND PENALTIES

An employee can go to court and ask that the transferee be ordered to pay damages for unfair dismissal. The employee can also ask to be reinstated in the transferee.

If the employee is dismissed by the transferor because of the transfer and/or if the transferee refuses to take on the employees, an employee can require that the transferee take over their contract which shall be deemed to have never been terminated.[55] If the new employer refuses to do so, the employee will be entitled to damages for unfair dismissal.[56] The employee can also ask to be incorporated in the new company[57] and to be compensated for the harm suffered as a result of their temporary removal from the company. The employee can also request the judicial termination of their contract in order to obtain payment of the salary that was due up until the judicial termination ruling, as well as severance pay and damages.[58] The employee can also claim damages from the transferor to compensate the harm suffered as a result of the termination of the contract.[59]

The employee can take legal action against his former employer or his new employer in order to establish their joint liability.

By way of exception to the above, when a job protection plan includes the transfer of one or several economic entities that is necessary to prevent the closure of one or several establishments and to safeguard employment, companies with more than 1,000 employees may dismiss some of the employees prior to the automatic transfer of the employment contracts.[60]

10.5.   CHECKLIST OF DOS AND DON'TS

– If the conditions for the transfer of an undertaking are met, the transferor should not dismiss the employees (except in certain number of limited cases) and the transferee should not oppose the transfer of the employment contracts.

---

55. Employment Chamber of the Court of Cassation, 20 Mar. 2002, *no. 00-41.651.*
56. Employment Chamber of the Court of Cassation, 19 Jan. 2010, *no. 08-45.002.*
57. Employment Chamber of the French Labour Code, 13 May 2009, *no. 07-44.671.*
58. Employment Chamber of the Court of Cassation, 2 Nov. 2005, *no. 03-45.215.*
59. Employment Chamber of the Court of Cassation, 19 May 2010, *no. 90-40.405.*
60. Section L. 1233-61 of the French Labour Code.

11.   EMPLOYEE REPRESENTATIVE BODIES

11.1.   OVERVIEW

Under French law, there are different employee representative bodies:
Staff delegates are mandatory in companies that have at least eleven employees.

A *works council* is mandatory in companies that have at least fifty employees. The works council must be informed or/and consulted on many economic, financial and professional matters. The employer must obtain the works council's opinion, whether positive or negative, on several legal or economic issues. In addition, the works council manages the social and cultural activities of the company or supervises the management of these activities.

A *health and safety committee* is set up in any establishment that has at least fifty employees. Its role is to involve the employees in actions for the prevention of professional risks and for the improvement of working conditions.

In companies with fewer than 300 employees, the employer may decide to set up a single staff representative body (*délégation unique du personnel*) whose duties and rights are those of the staff delegates, the works council, and of the health and safety committee combined. Moreover, in companies of more than 300 employees, a company-level majority collective agreement can provide for the grouping of two of, or all three of, the above-mentioned employee representative bodies.

When more than one of the above-mentioned employee representative bodies must be informed or consulted on a particular project, the employer may hold a joint meeting of these bodies pursuant to Sections L. 23-101-1 et seq. of the French Labour Code.

11.2.   WORKS COUNCIL

The works council can be set up at the level of the company when the latter does not have several establishments.

When the company has separate establishments with at least fifty employees, the works council is set up at the level of the establishment and a central works council is put in place at a company-wide level.

If the company is part of a group of companies, a group committee can also be set up at group level.

11.2.1.   The Setting up of the Works Council

The works council members and the staff delegates are elected by the employees of the company or the establishment in professional elections.

Employee representatives are elected for a four-year term unless a collective agreement provides for a term of between two and four years.

The number of representatives to be elected depends on the number of employees at the company or the establishment.

11.2.2. Composition of the Works Council

The works council is composed of the employer who is the president of the works council; members who are elected by the employees in the professional elections; a union representative for each trade union which obtained at least 10% of the votes in the last professional elections.

11.2.3. Meetings of the Works Council

The works council meets at least once every two months in companies with fewer than 300 employees and at least once per month in companies of 300 or more employees. Nevertheless, a second meeting can be held at the employer's initiative or at the request of the majority of its members.

The employer, as president of the works council, must invite all the works council members to the meeting and fix the date of the meeting.[61]

The meeting agenda is fixed by the employer and the secretary of the works council together. The compulsory consultations are automatically included on the agenda. The agenda is then sent to the works council at least three days before the meeting.

11.2.4. Economic Role of the Works Council

– *Scope of the Works Council Consultations*

Pursuant to section L. 2323-6 of the French Labour Code, the works council is informed and consulted each year on the three following topics:

– *the strategic orientations of the company;*
– *the economic and financial situation of the company;*
– *the company's social policy, the working conditions and employment.*

The works council must also be informed of and consulted in good time on a number of other questions. In particular, it is consulted on issues related to the *organization, management and operations of the company* (decisions

---

61. Employment Chamber of the Court of Cassation, 15 Jan. 2013, *no. 11-28.324.*

related to reductions in the workforce, structure of the workforce, working time, changes in the economic or legal organization of the company, professional training and apprenticeship programmes), the introduction of new technologies likely to affect notably employment and working conditions, restructuring and workforce reduction projects, changes in the company's legal or economic organization due notably to mergers and acquisitions and on *safeguard procedure, receivership or liquidation proceedings*.

In order for the works council to render an opinion on one of the above-mentioned topics, the works council must be consulted before the employer takes any decision. It must also be provided with all the necessary accurate and written information regarding the project, its reasons and justifications, terms and conditions and its consequences on employees. The works council must have enough time to analyse the information and must receive clear answers from the employer to all of its observations.

– *Defined Time Limits for the Works Council to render its opinion*

Section L. 2323-3 of the French Labour Code provides that the employer and the representative trade unions (or, failing that, the works council) can enter into an agreement that fixes the time limit for the works council to render its opinion. In any case, the time limit cannot be less than fifteen days.

If an agreement on the time limit cannot be reached, a decree has specified that the works council must give its opinion within the following time limits, calculated with effect from the employer's communication of the information required by the French Labour Code:

– one month generally;
– two months if the works council is assisted by an Expert;
– three months if one or more health and safety committee(s) (*CHSCTs*) are concerned by the project;
– four months if a temporary coordination committee of the health and safety committee is created (please refer to section 11.4.4).
– These time limits are applicable to the opinions to be delivered by the works council in the absence of any other time limit provided for by law.

If the works council has not rendered an opinion within the said time limit, it would be considered that the works council has been consulted and has rendered a negative opinion.

In addition, in some specific cases provided by law, in connection with its functions, the works council can appoint a certified public accountant to assist it.

If the works council considers that it has not been provided with enough information, it may go to court to obtain that the employer be ordered to provide the works council with all the relevant information. The judge takes a decision within eight days following the date of the application to the court.

However, it should be noted that such action does not extend the time limit for the works council to render its opinion.

Economic information to be provided to the Works Council

To carry out its role, the works council is provided with a certain amount of information by the employer.

First, after its election, the works council must be provided with economic and financial information in writing concerning, in particular, the legal form of the company and its organization, the company's business prospects, the position of the company within the group (as the case may be) and the capital distribution within shareholders holding more than 10% of the share capital.

The French Labour Code also provides that a single economic and social database must be created containing information regarding social investment (notably regarding employment, training and working conditions), tangible and intangible investments, share capital and debt, remuneration of employees and executives, social and cultural activity, financial flows for the company and notably state aid and tax credits, subcontracting, commercial and financial transfers between group companies.

The single economic and social database must also contain the information regularly provided by the employer to the health and safety committee.

This database is regularly updated and permanently accessible to the members of the works council, members of the health and safety committee, staff delegates (when their duties and rights are those of the works council) and union delegates.

Members of the works council and health and safety committee and trade union delegates are subject to a professional secrecy obligation regarding manufacturing processes and an obligation of discretion regarding the information it is provided with and that is confidential and presented as such by the employer (refer to section 20.2.1).

Within the framework of its economic role, the works council also benefits from an 'alert right' when it knows facts which may worryingly impact the economic situation of the company.

– *The role of Works Council when an employer contemplates closing an establishment*

When a company with at least 1,000 employees contemplates a collective redundancy plan that results in the closure of an establishment, the employer must look for a purchaser and provide a reasoned response to the relevant purchaser for each purchase offer received.

The employer has to inform, by any appropriate means, potential purchasers of its intention to sell the establishment. The employer also has to inform the works council and the Labour Authorities of the contemplated closure of the establishment. The employer must inform the works council that it is looking for a purchaser and any potential purchaser as soon as the employer is aware of such potential purchaser. The works council can render an opinion on the purchase offers (sections L. 1233-57-9 et seq. of the French Labour Code).

The works council can file a claim before the Commercial Court (*Tribunal de Commerce*) if the company refuses a purchase offer or if the employer has not complied with the above-mentioned obligations. Thus, the Commercial Court could order the company to reimburse the State subsidies received over the last two years, including business start-up, economic development or employee hiring subsidies.

11.2.5. Social Role of the Works Council

Pursuant to section L. 2323-83 of the French Labour Code, the works council ensures, controls or participates in the management of all social and cultural activities in the company in favour of the employees and their families.

11.3. STAFF DELEGATES

Staff delegates are elected at the company-level when the company has only one establishment. If the company has several establishments, the staff delegates are elected at each separate establishment.

11.3.1. The Setting Up of Staff Delegates and Number of Delegates

In principle, the elections of the works council and the staff delegates must take place at the same time. Refer to section 11.2.1 as the rules are strictly the same as for the works council.

The number of staff delegates depends on the number of employees at the company or establishment.

11.3.2. Meetings with the Staff Delegates

The staff delegates collectively meet with the employer at least once a month. They can also meet with the employer if they so request.

All the staff delegates must be invited to attend the meeting.

Two working days before the date of the meeting, the staff delegates communicate to the employer a written note setting out the object of the requests being presented. The employer must provide written answers to these requests, within six working days from the meeting. The employer must give reasons for the answers.

11.3.3.   Role of the Staff Delegates

General role: The staff delegates' general role is to present to the employer all the employees' individual or collective grievances related to wages, the application of the French Labour Code, and other legal provisions related to social protection, health and security, and the application of the collective agreements which apply in the company.

The staff delegates may also refer any matters to the Labour Inspector concerning any claims and comments related to the application of the legal provisions for which it has the responsibility of ensuring compliance.

Role in the absence of a works council: Pursuant to section L. 2313-15 of the French Labour Code, the staff delegates can communicate to the employer any suggestions aimed at improving the productivity and the general organization of the company. The staff delegates exercise the economic role of the works council.

They may also exercise their economic 'alert right' in the same conditions as the works council.

Role in the absence of the health and safety committee: The staff delegates carry out the role attributed to this committee.

11.4.   HEALTH AND SAFETY COMMITTEE

11.4.1.   The Setting Up of the Health and Safety Committee

A health and safety at work committee is compulsory in each establishment or company with at least fifty employees. If a company is only made up of establishments with fewer than fifty employees, a health and safety committee is compulsory in at least one of the establishments. All employees of these establishments shall be affiliated with a health and safety committee. In the absence of such a committee in an establishment of less than fifty employees, the employees of this establishment shall be affiliated with a health and safety committee of another establishment. In the absence of the health and safety committee in a company with more than fifty employees, the role of such committee is carried out by the staff delegates (please refer to section 11.3.3). The members of the health and safety committee are appointed by a body of electors composed of the members of the works council and the staff delegates. The number of members on the health and safety committee depends on the number of employees at the establishment. The members are appointed for a period of time which ends with the term of the elected works council members that appointed them, and they may be re-elected.

11.4.2. Composition of the Health and Safety Committee

The health and safety committee is composed notably of the employer who is the president of the committee, staff representatives and the occupational health doctor.

11.4.3. Meetings of the Health and Safety Committee

The agenda of the committee meetings is drafted by the president and the secretary of the committee.

The committee meets at least once a quarter at the initiative of the head of the establishment or further to any accident which resulted or might have resulted in serious consequences, or at the reasoned request of two members of the committee.

11.4.4. Role of the Health and Safety Committee

The health and safety committee participates in the protection of, and the prevention of risks related to the physical and mental health of the employees, their security and the improvement of their working conditions. The committee also analyses the professional risks, the working conditions and the exposure of the employees to 'arduous work' factors, can carry out inquiry and inspection assignments in order to check the employer complies with the regulations concerning working conditions and health and safety. It can also make proposals in the area of prevention and has an important consultative role. Generally, the committee is entitled to be consulted by the employer on all matters related to its remit.

In order for the health and safety committee to be able to carry out its role, the employer must provide the committee with all necessary information.

The committee can appoint an expert in the event of a major project altering the health and safety or working conditions and if a serious risk has been noted in the establishment.[62]

The committee is subject in the same conditions as the works council to obligations of professional secrecy and discretion.

Pursuant to section L. 4616-1 of the French Labour Code, in the event that a project involving major developments altering the health and safety and working conditions, and the introduction of new technologies, is common to several establishments, the employer can set up a temporary coordination body of the health and safety committee, whose remit consists of organizing an expert's investigation and rendering an opinion on the project. This coordination body is composed notably of the employer, representatives of each health and safety committee concerned by the project, the occupational health doctor and the labour inspector.

11.5. PROTECTION OF THE EMPLOYEE REPRESENTATIVES

Employee representatives, benefit from legal protection in connection with the performance and termination of their employment contract. They remain protected for six months after the end of their tenure (twelve months after the end of the tenure for the union delegate).

Therefore, the employer cannot impose on protected employees any substantial change to their employment contracts or any change in their working conditions.

To dismiss a protected employee, whatever the reason, the employer must consult the works council (or the staff delegates if there is no works council) on the contemplated dismissal and request from the Labour Authorities the authorization to dismiss the employee.

After the authorization, the employer can then notify the employee of their dismissal. If the authorization is refused, the employee must be maintained in their job with the same advantages.

11.6. FINES AND PENALTIES

Failure to consult or not properly consulting the works council may qualify as a criminal offence (*délit d'entrave*), such that the works council can be paid damages. The works council can also go to court to obtain that the company's planned transaction be suspended by the judge until the consultation

---

62. See section L. 4614-13 of the French Labour Code regarding the dispute of the expert's fees.

procedure is regularized. The employer can also be sentenced to one year's imprisonment and a EUR 7,500 fine if they hinder the appointment of the employee representatives or constitution of the employee representative bodies. The employer can be sentenced to a EUR 7,500 fine if they prevent the employee representatives from carrying out their duties.

Any dismissal without the authorization of the Labour Authorities is null and void.

11.7.   CHECKLIST OF DOS AND DON'TS

- An agreement with the members of the works council must be entered into in order to determine the deadline for the works council to issue its opinion on all consultation procedures required by the French Labour Code. Alternatively, separate agreements can be entered into for each consultation procedure in order to establish these deadlines.
- The employer must ensure that the employee representatives are able to carry out their role in order for the company not to be sued for discrimination or obstruction.

12.   TRADE UNIONS

12.1.   OVERVIEW

Unlike employees in other countries, French employees are not represented by just one trade union. They can be represented by several unions in the same company or industry sector.

Trade union rights in the company are exercised through the company-level union branch, the representative of the company-level union branch and the union delegate.

12.2.   'REPRESENTATIVENESS' OF THE UNIONS IN THE COMPANY

To be considered as representative, a trade union must demonstrate that it meets several of the following criteria, such as respecting republican values, being independent vis-à-vis the employer, applying financial transparency, being in existence for at least two years as regards the professional and geographical scope of the establishment or company, having obtained a certain number of votes in the professional elections, having a certain amount of influence through its activity and experience, and having a certain number of members and subscriptions.

12.3.   Trade Union Representation in the Company

12.3.1.   The Company-Level Union Branch

A company-level union branch is created when a union has at least two members and represents the material and moral interests of its members, pursuant to the objects of the union.

12.3.2.   The Union Delegate

In principle, a union delegate can be appointed only in companies or establishments of at least fifty employees. In companies of less than fifty employees, a staff delegate can be appointed as a union delegate.

Only trade unions that are representative can appoint a union delegate.

The tenure of the union delegate ends in principle when the terms of office of the employee representatives in the company end.

The main function of the union delegate is to negotiate and conclude collective agreements with the employer. The union delegate benefits from a protected status such that the disciplinary power of the employer is regulated and the termination of the employment contract is subject to the same procedure as that which applies to the works council members and the staff delegates (for more details, please refer to section 11.5).

The union delegate also benefits from legal provisions that prohibit discrimination based on union membership or activity.

12.3.3.   The Representative of the Company-Level Union Branch

The representative of the company-level union branch is an employee of the company appointed by a non-representative trade union to represent it in the company or the establishment. Their role is to lead the company-level union branch in order for the trade union which appointed them to obtain a result in the professional elections enabling it to be considered as representative.

Unless more favourable clauses in the collective bargaining agreement provide otherwise, a representative of the company-level union branch can be appointed only in companies or establishments of at least fifty employees. In companies of less than fifty employees, a staff delegate can be appointed as a representative of the company-level union branch.

This representative has the same rights as the union delegate, except, in principle, the right to negotiate and conclude collective agreements.

Their term of office ends, in principle, after the next professional elections that follow their appointment or in case of a significant and lasting fall in the headcount.

12.4.   FINES AND PENALTIES

Any decision based on discrimination due to union membership or activity is null and void.[63]

When the employer obstructs the appointment of a union delegate or prevents the union delegate from carrying out their duties, the employer may be liable on criminal grounds, such that the employer may be sentenced to a EUR 3,750 fine. Such acts can also qualify as hindering the exercise of trade union rights in the company.

12.5.   CHECKLIST OF DOS AND DON'TS

– The employer must not oppose the exercise of trade union rights in his company.

13.   COLLECTIVE BARGAINING

13.1.   OVERVIEW

Collective bargaining is defined as the discussion between employers' organizations or the employers themselves and employees' trade unions concerning employment, professional training and working conditions. The negotiation can lead to the conclusion of a collective bargaining agreement.

Collective bargaining agreements can be entered into at different levels: company or group level, at the level of each establishment or group of establishments, business combination, economic and social unit, professional or interprofessional.

13.2.   PARTIES TO THE NEGOTIATION

In principle, under French law, only employees' trade unions which are representative (for more details, please refer to 12.2) and which are represented

---

63.   Employment Chamber of the Court of Cassation, 4 Dec. 2001, *no. 99-43.231.*

by a union delegate can enter into a collective bargaining agreement with the employer.

When there are union delegates in the company, only they have the right to negotiate collective bargaining agreements.

In companies or establishments where there are no union delegates, the employer can negotiate and conclude collective bargaining agreements under certain conditions with employee representatives or employees empowered to negotiate.

13.3.   CONTENT OF A COLLECTIVE AGREEMENT

A collective agreement deals with all or one of the following matters: employment, professional training and working conditions.

Some clauses are mandatory. Indeed, the collective agreement must specify the applicable professional and territorial scope, the conditions under which it can be renewed or revised, the conditions under which indefinite-term collective agreements can be terminated.

With regard to the content of a collective agreement, one specific question has given rise to abundant case law decisions: can a collective agreement legitimately and effectively provide for benefits that are exclusively reserved for a specific category or group of employees or does such a provision violate the principle of equal treatment?

In 2009,[64] the Court of Cassation held, in a decision regarding additional days of paid leave to which exclusively executives were entitled by an in-house agreement, that the mere difference of professional category does not suffice to justify, as regards the granting of benefits, a difference in treatment amongst employees who are in an identical position with regard to the said benefit and concluded that such a difference needed to be justified by objective and pertinent reasons. This solution was heavily criticized by legal scholars, as it, de facto, threatened the lawfulness of numerous stipulations of collective bargaining agreements.

Six years later, by a series of decisions dated 27 January 2015,[65] the Court of Cassation has completely changed its position adopted in 2009. Hence, it has ruled that difference in treatment between professional categories provided for by collective agreements is presumed to be justified, shifting the burden of proof to the person wishing to challenge these differences and leaving such

---

64. Employment Chamber of the Court of Cassation, 1 Jul. 2009, *no. 07-42.675.*
65. Employment Chamber of the Court of Cassation, 27 Jan. 2015, *no. 13-22.179.* Also see subsequent case: Employment Chamber of the Court of Cassation, 8 Jun. 2016, *no. 15-11.324.*

person to show that these said differences are not motivated by professional reasons.

13.4.   TERM OF COLLECTIVE BARGAINING AGREEMENTS

Pursuant to section L. 2222-4 of the French Labour Code, a collective bargaining agreement can be concluded for an indefinite or a fixed term. Unless otherwise agreed, the collective bargaining has a term of five years.

13.5.   AMENDMENTS TO COLLECTIVE BARGAINING AGREEMENTS

According to section L. 2222-5 of the French Labour Code, agreements can be amended or supplemented.

An amendment which amends all or part of the initial agreement automatically replaces the provisions of the initial agreement and, provided it is filed with the Labour Authorities, is binding as against all the employees without them being able to claim that there has been a substantial amendment to their employment contracts.[66]

13.6.   REVOCATION OF COLLECTIVE BARGAINING AGREEMENTS

An indefinite-term agreement can be revoked by its signatories. The agreement itself provides for the conditions of such revocation, notably the length of the notice which must be given. In the absence of such an express clause, three months' notice must be given. The revocation must be notified by the initiator to the other signatories.

The revocation produces its effects only if all the signatories to the agreement agree to such revocation. Indeed, pursuant to section L. 2261-10 of the French Labour Code, when the agreement is revoked by all the signatories, a new negotiation must be undertaken within three months following the revocation if one of the parties so requests.

The revoked agreement remains applicable in whole either until a new agreement concluded after the revocation and replacing the revoked agreement enters into force, or, if such an agreement is not concluded, for one year following expiry of the notice period, unless a clause provides for a longer predefined term.

Pursuant to section L. 2261-13 of the French Labour Code, upon expiry of the one-year period following the notice, if the revoked agreement has not been

---

66. Employment Chamber of the Court of Cassation, 16 Nov. 1993, *no. 90-43.233.*

replaced by a new agreement, it no longer applies. However, the employees continue to benefit from an annual remuneration that may not be less than the salary paid within the last twelve months.

13.7. CHECKLIST OF DOS AND DON'TS

– It is highly recommended that all the trade unions which are representative in the company be invited to negotiate an agreement. Otherwise, the employer could be held liable for discrimination.

14. INDUSTRIAL ACTION

14.1. OVERVIEW

In France, there are two kinds of industrial action: strikes and lock-outs.

The right to strike is a right attributed to employees whereas the lock-out right is a right attributed to employers.

The right to strike is provided for by the French Constitution and the French Labour Code.

14.2. STRIKES

14.2.1. The Conditions for a Legal Strike

For an industrial dispute to qualify as a legal strike, the following conditions must be met:

A collective work stoppage: A strike is an individual right used collectively by the employees.

A coordinated work stoppage: Employees must stop working in a coordinated way with the common intent to support professional demands.

A complete work stoppage: A strike implies a complete stoppage of the work.

Length and form of the work stoppage: The length of the work stoppage is irrelevant. For example, a work stoppage lasting one hour can still be a strike.[67] Likewise, short and repeated stoppages, regardless of the disruption to production, constitute the normal exercise of the right to strike.[68]

---

67. Employment Chamber of the Court of Cassation, 29 Jan. 1960, *no. 58-40.507.*
68. Employment Chamber of the Court of Cassation, 25 Jan. 2011, *no. 09-69.030.*

Professional demands: The demands motivating a strike must be of a professional nature and be related to rights directly concerning the strikers. For example, professional demands related to wages and collective working hours.

14.2.2.   Limits on the Right to Strike

French law acknowledges several limits on the right to strike, such as the State being able to require the strikers to go back to work (in case of emergency), unlawful actions (i.e., actions that do not meet the criteria to qualify as a legal strike), abuse of the right to strike because of the circumstances in which the actions are led. There is an abuse of the right to strike if the strike results in or could result in disruption to the company itself,[69] but not just production.[70]

14.2.3.   Consequences of the Right to Strike

Exercising the right to strike suspends the employment contract and releases the employer and the employee of their respective obligations. In particular, the employer is exempted from paying remuneration to the employee.

In principle, the working hours that are lost because of a strike within the company cannot be made up.

In addition, the striker benefits from specific protection: he cannot be discriminated against. Moreover, except in the event of wilful misconduct (e.g., sequestration, destruction of the company's assets), the employer no longer has any disciplinary authority over strikers, such that the striker can be neither subject to disciplinary measures nor dismissed due to exercising, in a due and proper manner, the right to strike. Failing this, the dismissal is automatically null and void.

Pursuant to sections L. 1242-6 and L. 1251-10 of the French Labour Code, the employer is prohibited from hiring an employee under a 'precarious' employment contract to replace a striker. In the event of such hiring, the employer can be sentenced to a EUR 3,750 fine (and in case of a repeated offence to six months' imprisonment and a EUR 7,500 fine) and the employee's contract can be requalified as an indefinite-term contract.

---

69. Employment Chamber of the Court of Cassation, 11 Jan. 2000, *no. 97-18.215.*
70. Employment Chamber of the Court of Cassation, 7 Apr. 1993, *no. 91-16.834.*

14.2.4.   Fines and Penalties

Strikers and trade unions may be liable on civil or criminal grounds for unlawful actions committed in the context of a strike.

14.3.   Lock-Out

A lock-out is defined by case law as the temporary closure of a company, establishment or shop in the context of a strike. It is not acknowledged in substantive law.

According to case law, a lock-out is unlawful if it is a preventive measure or a retaliation measure with respect to the strike such that employers must compensate the employees for the loss of salary unless the employers can justify an unavoidable situation that prevented them from providing the employees with work. However, a lock-out is lawful when it is justified by the disruption to the company caused by an abuse of the right to strike that makes any business activity impossible[71] or a complete paralysis of the company resulting from the strike of the production department.[72] A lock-out is also lawful if it is justified by employees' safety or security of equipment.

Whether or not it is lawful, the lock-out results in the suspension of the employment contracts.

Except where the lock-out is lawful, the employer must pay the non-strikers during a strike (or all the employees in case of an anticipated lock-out) compensation in lieu of the salary lost.

14.4.   Checklist of Dos and Don'ts

– During strikes, an employer can deduct days not worked from the employees' salary provided that the days deducted correspond strictly to the duration of the work stoppage.

---

71. Employment Chamber of the Court of Cassation, 5 Jul. 1995, *no. 93-20.402.*
72. Employment Chamber of the Court of Cassation, 22 Feb. 2005, *no. 02-45.879.*

15. WORKING CONDITIONS: HOURS OF WORK AND PAYMENT OF WAGES: BY STATUTE OR COLLECTIVE AGREEMENTS

15.1. MINIMUM WAGE

The parties freely determine the structure and amount of remuneration paid to the employee in exchange for their work.[73] This freedom to fix the salary is nonetheless subject to several restrictions: the minimum wage set out in the collective bargaining agreement, legislation on overtime, the prohibition of indexation clauses, prohibited discrimination and the legal minimum wage.

As of 1 January 2017, the legal minimum wage is EUR 9.76 per hour.

Specific minimum wage provisions are also included in most industry-wide collective bargaining agreements on the basis of the level of the employees' job as defined by the collective bargaining agreement (known as the 'job coefficient'). The rates are usually increased annually.

15.2. MAXIMUM LENGTHS OF WORKING TIME AND REST PERIODS

15.2.1. Maximum Daily and Weekly Lengths of Working Time

The maximum number of hours that may be worked is forty-eight hours for any specific week or forty-four hours per week on average over a period of twelve consecutive weeks (sections L. 3121-20 and L. 3121-22 of the French Labour Code). Daily working time may not exceed ten hours (section L. 3121-18 of the French Labour Code). These maximum working hours per day and per week are subject to exemptions in certain circumstances.

15.2.2. Mandatory Rest Periods

Employees are in principle entitled to a daily rest period of at least eleven consecutive hours in each twenty-four hour working period (section L. 3131-1 of the French Labour Code).

The law prohibits employees from working more than six days a week, and employees are normally entitled to an uninterrupted rest period of at least twenty-four hours in each seven-day period, on top of which must be added the daily rest period of eleven hours, therefore resulting in a total uninterrupted weekly rest period of thirty-five hours. In principle, this weekly rest period must be granted on a Sunday (sections L. 3132-1 et seq. of the French Labour Code).

---

73. Employment Chamber of the Court of Cassation, 12 Mar. 1987, *no. 84-41.390.*

15.3. PART-TIME WORK

15.3.1. General Provisions

Under French law, a part-time worker is an employee working less than thirty-five hours per week or less than the working time specified in the collective bargaining agreement.

Such contracts must be in writing and must include certain mandatory provisions (in particular in respect of the number of hours worked per week/month, the arrangements for communicating the scheduling of hours worked per week/month and the maximum number of additional hours that the employee can work per month) (section L. 3123-6 of the French Labour Code).

In case of non-compliance with regulations on part-time employment, employees may seek to obtain that their part-time employment contracts be requalified as full-time employment contracts and obtain back pay and damages.

Part-time employees benefit from the same rights granted to full-time employees by law and by collective bargaining agreements unless otherwise specified within the collective agreement itself.

Part-time employees benefit from a priority right to obtain a full-time employment contract.

15.3.2. Minimum Duration Obligation

A company-wide agreement may provide for a minimum weekly working time. If no agreement has been signed, the applicable minimum weekly working time is of twenty-four hours per week (sections L. 3121-7, L. 3123-19 and L. 3123-27 of the French Labour Code). The company-wide agreement may also provide for compensation for the additional hours worked as from the first additional hour (see section 15.4.1 below). All employment contracts that last more than seven days and entered into from 1 July 2014 onwards must comply with this regulation. However, exceptions are allowed.

In accordance with section L. 3123-7 of the said Code, it is possible, upon the employee's written and substantiated request, to provide for working time which is less than the working time provided for in section L. 3123-27 of the French Labour Code, notably in order to allow the employee to deal with personal constraints.

The French Labour Code also provides for the possibility to sign an addendum to the part-time employment contract in order to temporarily increase the length of the weekly working time (section L. 3123-22 of the French Labour Code).

In addition, the section L. 2241-13 of the French Labour Code imposes on employers having at least one-third of their workforce as part-time employees to negotiate with the trade unions regarding the terms and conditions of part-time work (minimum weekly working time, modification of working hours, compensation for overtime, etc.).

15.4. OVERTIME

15.4.1. Overtime and Additional Hours

Although French working time is limited to thirty-five hours per week, this is merely a threshold over which overtime must be paid and/or compensatory rest provided.

Hours worked in excess of thirty-five hours per week are typically considered overtime (sections L. 3121-27 and L. 3121-28 of the French Labour Code).

The employer can also have a part-time employee work more than the contractually stipulated working hours (sections L. 3123-8 et seq. of the French Labour Code). These extra hours are referred to as 'additional hours' *(heures complémentaires)*.

Unless otherwise agreed in a company-wide agreement, any additional hour worked within the limit of 1/10th of the weekly or monthly working hours is paid at an increased rate of 10% (section L. 3123-29 of the French Labour Code). The 25% increase rate still applies to each hour worked in excess of the contractual amount, unless an industry-wide collective agreement provides for a lower rate, which may not be less than 10% (section L. 3123-21 of the French Labour Code).

15.4.2. Quota for Overtime Hours

All employers are subject to an annual overtime quota that is established by a company agreement or industry-wide collective agreement. If there is no such overtime agreement, the applicable quota is 220 hours per year per employee (section D. 3121-14-1, paragraph 1, of the French Labour Code).

15.4.3. Compensation and Time Off in Lieu

Overtime is paid at the hourly rate plus 25% for each of the first eight overtime hours, i.e., from the thirty-sixth to the forty-third hour, and the hourly rate plus 50% for each hour as from the forty-fourth hour. A company agreement or an industry-wide collective agreement can provide for a different rate, but it must not be less than 10% (section L. 3121-33 of the French Labour Code).

The payment of overtime may be replaced in whole or in part by equivalent time off in lieu.

15.5. EXEMPTIONS TO WAGE AND WORKING HOUR LAWS

15.5.1. Exemptions Regarding Top-Level Executives (*cadres dirigeants*)

Section L. 3111-2 of the French Labour Code defines a top-level executive as an employee: (i) who has broad responsibilities resulting in significant independence in the organization of his working time, (ii) with autonomous decision-making powers and (iii) whose level of remuneration is among the highest in the company.

If the above conditions are met, an employee qualified as a top-level executive is exempted from the regulations applicable to working time, in particular as regards maximum working hours and payment of overtime.

Consequently, the employee's compensation is a fixed sum, unrelated to the company's collective working hours or the employee's actual working hours and is not subject to any readjustment or any increase, of whatever nature it may be, relating to the number of hours actually worked by the employee.

15.5.2. Exemptions Regarding Employees under All-Inclusive Remuneration Agreement (*convention de forfait*)

Employers can enter into an all-inclusive remuneration agreement (*convention de forfait*) with their employees, pursuant to which the parties agree on a lump-sum remuneration that covers all hours of work that will be performed, without any distinction between ordinary or overtime hours (sections L. 3121-53 et seq. of the French Labour Code). All-inclusive remuneration agreements can provide for a fixed number of working hours per week, per month or over the year, or for a fixed number of days over the year. In all cases, the employee must give his consent to such an agreement in writing.

15.6. WORKING TIME BASED ON A NUMBER OF WORKING DAYS PER YEAR (*FORFAIT JOURS ANNUEL*)

15.6.1. Definition

Under French working time regulations, which provide for a legal average working week of thirty-five hours, certain autonomous executives can be subject to working time clauses which provide for a fixed maximum number of working days per year.

Such working time calculated in days may only apply to executives who have a significant amount of autonomy in the organization of their work schedule and who cannot be subject to the collective working time in view of their duties.

These executives are subject to working time calculated in days, i.e., the length of work is not expressed in terms of hours worked but in terms of days worked per year. They work a maximum number of days and receive a lump-sum salary in return. In such case, employees cannot claim overtime.

15.6.2.   Implementation and Requirements

Such scheme can be established in a company only if (i) a mandatory national branch-level collective bargaining agreement and/or a company-level collective bargaining agreement provide(s) for this possibility and (ii) the relevant employees have an individual addendum to their employment contract or a specific clause in their employment contract.

In addition, the Court of Cassation has ruled in a number of cases that the collective agreement (i) must provide for guarantees ensuring that working hours and the workload remain reasonable and (ii) provides for safeguards in respect of the protection of the health and safety of the employees. Failing which, the days-per-year all-inclusive agreement is not binding and rules related to overtime apply.[74,75,76,77]

The 2016 Labour law reform has codified this case law and requires from now on that the collective agreement must set out provisions on how (i) the employer monitors the employee's workload, (ii) the employee and the employer communicate about the employee's workload, the balance between working and private lives and his/her remuneration and (iii) the employee may exercise his/her right to disconnect from technology (section L. 3121-64 of the French Labour Code). In the absence of such provisions, the French Labour Code provides for measures applicable by default.

Moreover, the employer must ensure that the employee's workload remains reasonable and that there is an appropriate work allocation.

The employee may agree in writing to waive part of his time off and work more than 218 days (subject to an overall maximum of 235 days per year), in exchange for an increase in salary, with the additional days worked being remunerated by additional compensation representing at least 110% of the base salary. Such consent must be renewed each year.

---

74. Employment Chamber of the Court of Cassation, 4 Feb. 2015, *no. 13-20.891.*
75. Employment Chamber of the Court of Cassation, 29 Jun. 2011, *no. 09-71.107.*
76. Employment Chamber of the Court of Cassation, 31 Jan. 2012, *no. 10-19.807.*
77. Employment Chamber of the Court of Cassation, 26 Sep. 2012, *no. 11-14.540.*

15.6.3.   Sanctions

In case of violation of these requirements, the all-inclusive agreement will thereafter be deemed to be invalid.[78] Therefore, executives whose working time is calculated in days per year could claim that they should be subject to the collective working time, i.e., thirty-five hours per week and as a consequence: employees would be entitled to claim overtime for hours worked over thirty-five hours per week for the past three years, plus damages for non-compliance with the maximum working time limits based on the harm suffered. Regarding the proof of hours worked, the Court of Cassation has consistently ruled that the burden of proof does not entirely and exclusively lay with the employee, but is in fact shared with the employer: it is the responsibility of the employee to substantiate their claims, enabling the employer to respond by bringing forward their own evidence.[79]

Failure to comply with overtime legal requirements (not declaring and/or not paying all hours may be construed as undeclared work (*travail dissimulé*). In this respect, an employer could be sentenced to a EUR 225,000 fine (three years' imprisonment and a EUR 45,000 fine for the legal representatives of the company).

By way of exception to the above, if the collective bargaining agreement does not comply with the legal requirements, the 2016 Labour law reform allows the employer to avoid civil and criminal sanctions if he voluntarily applies the legal requirements (section 12, Law no. 2016-1088, 8 August 2016).

15.7.   NIGHT WORK

15.7.1.   Definition

'Night time' means the hours between 9 pm and 6 am, unless otherwise provided for by a company-level or an industry-wide collective agreement. A night worker is a worker who works at least three hours of their daily working time at night at least twice a week or who carries out a certain number of hours of night time work over the reference period as defined by the applicable collective bargaining agreement.

Generally speaking, the daily working time of a night worker may not exceed eight hours, and the weekly working time may not exceed forty hours over a period of twelve consecutive weeks.

---

78.   Employment Chamber of the Court of Cassation, 29 Jun. 2011, *no. 09-71.107.*
79.   Employment Chamber of the Court of Cassation, 30 Sep. 2014, *no. 13-14.707.*

15.7.2. Implementation

Under French law, night work (any work carried out between 9 pm and 6 am) must be justified by the necessity of ensuring that the economic activity or the public services provided by the company continue.

Night work cannot be implemented by the employer's unilateral decision. It must be implemented by a collective bargaining agreement, or authorized by the labour inspector.

The collective bargaining agreement must contain all the compulsory clauses (type of position, justification for night work, compensatory rest, or where appropriate, compensation in the form of salary).

The implementation of night work in violation of the legal provisions constitutes a manifestly unlawful act (*trouble manifestement illicite*). In a decision of 24 September 2014, the Court of Cassation ruled that implementing night work in a sector (in the case at hand the perfumery sector) where night work is not inherent to the activity constitutes such a manifestly unlawful act.[80]

15.7.3. Sanctions

Failure to comply with legislation on night work and weekly rest constitutes a criminal offence, and is also subject to civil sanctions:

Criminal sanctions: The company can be fined up to EUR 7,500 (EUR 1,500 for its legal representatives). This fine is due for each offence and for each employee affected.

Civil sanctions: Employees working at night may claim both back pay (equal to additional compensation or equivalent compensatory rest they should have received) and damages (on the basis of the harm suffered by them).

15.8. Reductions in Compensation Caused by Economic Downturn

In the case of a difficult economic context entailing, for instance, a reduction in the workload, the employer can reduce working time, or temporarily stop operations and implement short-time work, also referred to as a 'partial activity' scheme (*activité partielle*), after having complied with a specific procedure (in particular consulting the works council and requesting the authorization of the French administration). In this respect, communication between the employer and the French labour authorities is completely dematerialized and

---

80. Employment Chamber of the Court of Cassation, 24 Sep. 2014, *no. 13-24.851.*

employers are obliged to join an internet-based service managed by the Agency for Services and Payment (*Agence de services et de paiement, or ASP*).[81]

According to section L. 5122-1 of the French Labour Code, such a scheme applies:

- In the event of a temporary closure of a business or part of the business (where recovery is expected in the short-term).
- In the case of a reduction of working time to below the legal working time.

According to section L. 5122-1 of the French Labour Code, when the conditions for short-time work are fulfilled, the employees receive specific compensation from the employer corresponding to 70% of the monthly gross remuneration (section R. 5122-18 of the French Labour Code). In addition, the employer receives a partial activity allowance, financed by the State and unemployment insurance. The hourly allowance rate is fixed at EUR 7.74 for companies with fewer than 250 employees, and EUR 7.23 above that (section D. 5122-13 of the French Labour Code).

15.9. CHECKLIST OF DOS AND DON'TS

- The employer must comply with certain obligations regarding working conditions, otherwise there is the risk that the employer will encounter individual or collective conflicts with the employees. Remuneration and working time are two pillars of French labour law.

16. OTHER WORKING CONDITIONS AND BENEFITS PROVIDED FOR BY LAW, COLLECTIVE BARGAINING AGREEMENTS OR COMPANY POLICY

16.1. HEALTH AND OTHER INSURANCE

As from 1 January 2016, all employees must be covered by private health insurance. If employers have not provided such private health insurance by that date, they must set up by unilateral decision a minimal health insurance.

16.2. PENSION AND RETIREMENT BENEFITS

Supplementary company pension plans can be set up in addition to the basic social security regime and the obligatory complementary schemes.

---

81. Article 6 of Decree of 30 Jun. 2014.

16.3.   PAID LEAVE AND HOLIDAY PAYMENTS

16.3.1.   Annual Paid Leave Entitlement

Unless the applicable collective bargaining agreement provides for more favourable treatment, French employees have five weeks of paid leave per year, and any additional 'RTT' days (*reduction du temps de travail*; these days off are granted when employees work beyond the thirty-five-hour working week) that may have been negotiated when the thirty-five-hour working week took effect.

Public holidays are not included as part of an employee's annual leave entitlement.

16.3.2.   Paid Leave upon Termination of the Employment Contract

In the case of dismissal, the employer must pay the employee for all accrued leave not taken.

16.4.   LEAVE OF ABSENCE

Apart from paid leave under French law, employees may benefit from other leaves such as leave for personal reasons, sick leave, bereavement leave, family leave, pregnancy leave, maternity leave.

16.5.   INJURY AT WORK

Pursuant to section L. 433-1 of the Social Security Code, in the event of a work accident, employees are entitled to their full salary from the first day of absence. Payment for the day of work during which the accident occurred is the responsibility of the employer. Compensation ceases on the date on which the injury heals or is stabilized, or upon the death of the employee. The amount of sick pay per day (*indemnité journalière*) is 60% of the basic salary per day for the first twenty-eight days, and 80% of the basic salary for each day thereafter. The applicable collective bargaining agreement can provide that the employer will make up the difference in full or in part.

The French Social Security Code requires that the employer report any accident suffered at work to the health insurance body.

16.6.   CHECKLIST OF DOS AND DON'TS

– It is prohibited to discriminate against an employee due to health reasons or because an employee is pregnant.

17.   WORKERS' COMPENSATION

17.1.   OVERVIEW

French law compensates employees who suffer work accidents. To be qualified as such, the accident must have occurred at the place of work. If the employee works from home, the accident can still qualify as a work accident if the employee was working at the time of the accident.

The injured employee must file a declaration within twenty-four hours of the accident (sections L. 441-1 et seq. of the Social Security Code). The employee must also have their injury acknowledged by a doctor on a work accident form. Once the accident has been declared, the victim is entitled to receive the benefits paid by the State health insurance fund (*caisse d'assurance maladie*).

The employee's employment contract is suspended until they have made a complete recovery. An employer cannot dismiss an employee who is absent due to a work accident. Only serious misconduct by the employee, or a situation where it is impossible to continue the contract for reasons unrelated to the accident, can justify termination of employment (section L. 1226-9 of the French Labour Code).

After the period of suspension, the employee is entitled to return to the position that they held previously if the occupational health doctor finds that they are fit to fulfil the duties of the position. If the position no longer exists or is no longer vacant, the employee has to be reinstated in a similar position with an equivalent salary (section L. 1226-8, paragraph 1, of the French Labour Code).

If the occupational health doctor concludes that the employee is unfit to return to their position, the employer must, after having obtained the opinion of the employee representatives, offer the employee another job that is adapted to their physical condition. The job offer should take into account the written conclusions of the occupational health doctor. If it is impossible to reinstate the employee, they can be dismissed (section L. 1226-2 of the French Labour Code).

17.2. CHECKLIST OF DOS AND DON'TS

– Do not dismiss an employee due to a workplace injury.
– Reinstate the employee upon expiry of the period of suspension of their employment contract.

18. COMPANY'S OBLIGATION TO PROVIDE A SAFE AND HEALTHY WORKPLACE

18.1. REQUIREMENTS

The employer is bound by a duty to take reasonable care of the employees' health and safety. This duty in respect of health and safety is particularly onerous on the employer.

In 2002, the Court of Cassation ruled that the obligation to ensure the employees' safety is an *absolute obligation* (*obligation de résultat*).[82]

Employers must evaluate the risks inherent in their company in order to put preventive measures in place if necessary (sections L. 4121-1 et seq. of the French Labour Code). Work and production methods must protect the health and safety of workers.

Employers are under an obligation to take all appropriate measures (such as risk prevention, training, the provision of information, etc.) to protect the health and safety of their employees. Employers are obliged to carry out risk assessments and then advise their employees of any known or potential risks associated with their job and the preventative measures to be taken to eliminate or minimize the dangers associated with those risks. More precisely, according to section R. 4121-1 of the French Labour Code, employers must transcribe and update the results of the professional risks assessment and factors of 'arduous work' in a single document, the so-called *'document unique'*.

As from 1 January 2016, in principle, each year employers must draw up a list of the employees exposed to professional risks. It will be transmitted to the pension funds in charge of the 'arduous work' account (*compte pénibilité*). Failure to comply with legislation concerning the *'document unique'* is subject to criminal and civil sanctions. The company can be fined up to EUR 7,500. Employees may claim damages if there is no 'document unique'.[83]

As from 1 January 2017, each employee has a 'personal account of activity' (*compte personnel d'activité*) which combines, as a first step, the 'arduous work' account (*compte pénibilité*) and the personal training account (*compte personnel de formation*).

---

82. Employment Chamber of the Court of Cassation, 11 Apr. 2002, *no. 00-16.535.*
83. Employment Chamber of the Court of Cassation, 8 Jul. 2014, *no. 13-15.47 and 13-15.474*

The employer's obligation to provide a healthy and safe working environment is obviously an absolute obligation in the event of the employee's exposure to carcinogenic substances present within the workplace, such as asbestos. In this respect, the Court of Cassation ruled in 2010[84] that the employee's mere exposure to asbestos entitles them to claim financial compensation from their employer for the anxiety associated with the development of serious diseases. In other words, in its decision of 11 May 2010, the Court of Cassation acknowledged the existence of a special kind of prejudice: the specific prejudice of anxiety (*'préjudice spécifique d'anxiété'*).

Recently, the Court of Cassation has specifically limited entitlement to this financial compensation for having sustained the prejudice of anxiety. In a series of decisions dated 3 March 2015,[85] the Court of Cassation has held that only employees who have been exposed to asbestos present within companies mentioned on a specific list may be entitled to the compensation called the 'asbestos workers' anticipated cessation of activity allowance' (*allocation de cessation anticipée d'activité des travailleurs de l'amiante, or Acaata*).

18.2.   EMPLOYEES' RIGHTS

Pursuant to section L. 4131-1 of the French Labour Code, employees must immediately alert their employer of any work situation which they have reasonable grounds to believe presents a serious and imminent danger to their life or health, as well as any defect which they see in the protection systems. In addition, employees are entitled to leave a work situation which they have reasonable grounds to think presents a serious and imminent danger to their life or health, without having to obtain the prior approval of their employer. They can leave their work station without incurring disciplinary sanctions. Section L. 4131-3 of the French Labour Code states that employees who exercise their 'right to leave' (*droit de retrait*) must not suffer any salary deduction.

Employees are also entitled to ask the CHSCT to intervene and exercise its 'right to alert' (sections L. 4131-2 and L. 4132-2 to 4 of the French Labour Code).

18.3.   EMPLOYER'S RIGHTS

Employees must comply with the health and safety instructions given to them by their employer (section L. 4122-1 of the French Labour Code).

---

84. Employment Chamber of the Court of Cassation, 11 May 2010, *no. 09-42.241.*
85. Employment Chamber of the Court of Cassation, 3 Mar. 2015, *no. 13-20.474.*

Employees must take care of their health and safety at work, as well as the health and safety of other employees. An employer can take disciplinary action against an employee who does not comply with the health and safety instructions.

The employer can, however, assign the employee to another position commensurate with their skills and experience.

18.4. INJURY OR ACCIDENT AT WORK

Under French law, an accident that takes place during the employee's working hours and at the workplace is presumed to be a work accident. As soon as the State health insurance fund (*caisse primaire d'assurance maladie*) becomes aware of the accident, it must conduct interviews in order to determine whether the accident indeed occurred and whether it qualifies as a work accident.

The State health insurance fund has thirty days from the date it received the work accident report and the initial medical certificate to review the matter and determine whether it was a work accident or not.

If the State health insurance fund finds that the employer was liable, the fund must give the employer notice of its decision and explain the possible means of recourse available and the respective deadlines for these procedures.

18.5. FINES AND PENALTIES

If an employer knew about a danger and did nothing to prevent it, this could constitute gross negligence if a breach of the obligation to ensure the employees' safety causes an injury to an employee. The employee can be awarded increased compensation for the employer's gross negligence. Moreover, the employer will pay more social contributions. Penal sanctions for breach of health and safety law can also be applied.

18.6. CHECKLIST OF DOS AND DON'TS

– Take preventive measures to ensure the health and safety of employees.

19. IMMIGRATION, SECONDMENT AND FOREIGN ASSIGNMENT

19.1. OVERVIEW OF LAWS CONTROLLING IMMIGRATION

Citizens of European countries, the European Economic Area and Switzerland benefit from provisions relating to the free movement of workers in Europe pursuant to Article 48 of the Treaty on the Functioning of the European Union.

Non-European citizens must have a valid permit authorizing them to work in France. A residence permit is valid for a period of ten years, is automatically renewable and allows the person to work in metropolitan France without any professional limitations. A temporary residence permit is issued for precise, professional purposes. Its period of validity varies according to the nature of the foreign employee's contract.

19.2. RECRUITING, SCREENING AND HIRING PROCESS

The hiring process differs depending on whether the foreigner resides in France or not.

If the foreigner resides in France, the employer must check with the Prefecture of the place of hiring that the worker's permit is valid, unless the foreigner is registered on the list of job seekers.

If the foreigner does not reside in France, the employer must file a job offer with the national job centre (*Pôle Emploi*) and look for locally qualified candidates. If no unemployed person is qualified, the employer files a request to introduce a foreign worker with the Regional Labour Authority (*Direction régionale des entreprises, de la concurrence, de la consommation, du travail et de l'emploi - DIRECCTE*).

19.3. OBLIGATION OF THE EMPLOYER TO ENFORCE IMMIGRATION LAWS

When an employer hires a foreigner, he must record the type and reference number of the permit authorizing the foreigner to work in France in the personnel ledger. Copies of the relevant documents must be annexed to the ledger.

19.4. FINES AND PENALTIES

Hiring a foreign worker who does not have a work permit authorizing them to carry out a salaried activity in France is subject to up to five years' imprisonment and/or a fine of up to EUR 15,000 for the representative of the company and up to EUR 75,000 for the company. The fine is applied for each foreigner employed. Additional penalties can be ordered by the courts.

Failure to verify that the foreigner has a work permit, failure to file the obligatory nominative declaration, or employing the services of a foreigner without verifying the geographical or professional restrictions of the person's work permit is subject to a fine of up to EUR 1,500 for the representative of the company and up to EUR 7,500 for the company.

In addition, such employment contract would be deemed to be null and void.

19.5.   SECONDMENT/FOREIGN ASSIGNMENT

When a French employee is sent abroad on assignment, the employer must ensure that the employee has the visas, residence and work permits required by the legislation of the country to which he is seconded. The employer must also obtain information about sanitary conditions in the country and make arrangements for the employee to undergo the obligatory vaccinations before leaving on secondment. A pre-secondment medical examination is also necessary so that the occupational health doctor can ensure that the employee is fit to travel and work abroad.

The parties are free to determine the governing law of the employment contract, provided that they comply with the mandatory rules of the objectively applicable law. If the parties have not determined the governing law of the contract, the governing law is in principle (i) that of the country in which, or from which, the employee habitually performs their work (even in the case of a temporary secondment), or if the governing law cannot be determined on this basis; (ii) the law of the country in which the company that hired the employee is located. However, if the circumstances are such that the employment contract has stronger ties with another country, then the law of this other country will govern the employment relationship.

Moreover, regardless of the law chosen by the parties and/or the objectively applicable law governing the employment contract, certain imperative rules of the local legislation have to be applied.

In addition, where a parent company puts one of its employee at the disposal of a foreign subsidiary and an employment contract is concluded between the employee and the subsidiary, the parent company must ensure that the employee will be repatriated in the event of their dismissal by the foreign subsidiary and that this employee will hold a similar position corresponding to their skills and responsibilities previously held within the parent company (section L. 1231-5 of the French Labour Code).

19.6.   SECURED VOLUNTARY MOBILITY

Sections L. 1222-12 to L. 1222-16 provide that in companies or groups of companies with at least 300 employees, an employee who has a minimum of twenty-four months' length of service can benefit from secured voluntary mobility (*mobilité volontaire sécurisée*) in order to carry out another activity in another company. During the period of mobility, their employment contract is suspended. The employee and the original employer enter into an amendment to the employment contract that provides for the object, the duration, and the start and end dates of the period of mobility, the notice period within which the employee must inform, in writing, their employer of their decision not to return to the company, the terms and conditions for the employee's return before the intended date. In any case, the employee can return at any time to the company with the agreement of the employer.

Once the employee has returned to the company, they are automatically reinstated in their previous position or a similar position with the same qualification, remuneration and classification.

In the event the employee chooses not to come back in their company at the end of mobility period, the employment contract concluded with the first employer is terminated and this termination is deemed to be a resignation.

Every six months the employer must communicate to the works council the list of employees having requested to benefit from secured voluntary mobility and the situation concerning such requests.

19.7.   CHECKLIST OF DOS AND DON'TS

– Check the validity of a foreign worker's residence permit before hiring a foreign worker.
– Comply with the declaration obligations.

20.   RESTRICTIVE COVENANTS, PROTECTION OF TRADE SECRETS AND CONFIDENTIAL INFORMATION AND NON-COMPETE AGREEMENTS

20.1.   OVERVIEW

Pursuant to section 1104 of the French Civil Code and section L. 1222-1 of the French Labour Code, an employment contract must be performed in good faith, i.e., the employee must refrain from any act contrary to the company's interests. The Court of Cassation has inferred from these provisions that employees have a general obligation of loyalty and discretion when performing their employment contract, and also after termination of the contract. This general obligation of loyalty covers confidentiality, professional secrecy, non-disclosure of trade secrets and non-compete obligations.

20.2. CONFIDENTIALITY, PROFESSIONAL SECRECY AND TRADE SECRETS

Protected employees (section 20.2.1 below) and ordinary employees (section 20.2.2 below) are bound by a duty of discretion and confidentiality vis-à-vis the employer.

20.2.1. Protected Employees

Works council members are privy to sensitive information regarding the health of the company, how it operates, manufacturing processes, etc. The members of the works council and the union representatives are subject to both professional secrecy and confidentiality obligations.

Violation of professional secrecy gives rise to criminal penalties: one year's imprisonment and/or a fine of up to EUR 15,000.

Furthermore, works council members and union representatives are subject to an obligation of discretion regarding information which is confidential and presented as such by the employer (section L. 2325-5 of the French Labour Code). Works council members cannot disclose confidential information to persons who are not official recipients of the information.

Breach of the obligation of discretion by works council members and union representatives exclusively results in civil liability and is not subject to criminal penalties contrary to violation of professional secrecy. The employer can also take disciplinary action against protected employees who disclose such information expressly marked as confidential,[86] including dismissal.

However, according to recent case law of French lower courts, documents remitted to the works council members cannot be marked as confidential in their entirety,[87,88] and if he does so, the employer may be subject to sanctions for abuse of the obligation of discretion.[89]

---

86. Employment Chamber of the Court of Cassation, 6 Mar. 2012, *no. 10-24.367.*
87. Court of First Instance of Lyon, 9 Jul. 2012, *no. 12/01153.*
88. Paris Court of Appeal, 11 Mar. 2013, *no. 12/20238.*
89. Employment Chamber of the Court of Cassation, 5 Nov. 2014, *no. 13-17.270.*

20.2.2. Ordinary Employees

Ordinary employees (i.e., employees who are not 'protected' employees) are subject to an obligation of loyalty and discretion towards their employer. Thus they cannot disclose, whether within or outside of the company, confidential information or knowledge obtained while performing their duties, such obligation being stricter for top executives. They are also prohibited from disclosing manufacturing secrets.

Breach of the obligation of discretion by ordinary employees may result in civil liability in case of gross misconduct and may give rise to criminal penalties: a fine of up to EUR 30,000 and/or up to two years' imprisonment (section L. 1227-1 of the French Labour Code). Violation of this duty of discretion can also trigger disciplinary action against ordinary employees, including dismissal.

20.3. NON-COMPETE UNDERTAKINGS

Under a non-compete clause, an employee agrees not to carry out, on his own behalf or on behalf of another employer, an activity similar to that of his employer's during a certain period of time following the termination of the employment relationship. A non-compete clause thus applies after the termination of the contractual relationship.

To be valid, a non-compete clause must be limited in time, geographically and in terms of the prohibited activities, and be necessary to protect the legitimate interests of the company, i.e., must be justified by the nature of the employee's duties and must not prevent the employee from finding work corresponding to their qualifications. It must also include financial compensation for the employee during the period of the non-compete obligation[90] which is a lump-sum compensation. Any non-compete clause that does not comply with these cumulative requirements is null and void, and therefore is not binding on the employee, and necessarily causes harm to the employee.[91,92]

Subject to this possibility being expressly provided for in the employment contract or in the collective bargaining agreement or expressly agreed by the employee, the employer can release the employee from their non-compete obligation on termination of their employment contract, subject to certain conditions. Even if there is established case law that the employer has the possibility to release the employee from their non-compete obligation on termination of their employment contract, the Court of Cassation has recently ruled that the

90. Employment Chamber of the Court of Cassation, 10 Jul. 2002, *no. 00-45.135.*
91. Employment Chamber of the Court of Cassation, 12 Jan. 2011, *no. 08-45.280.*
92. Employment Chamber of the Court of Cassation, 10 May 2012, *no. 09-72.348.*

possibility to release the employee from their non-compete obligation *whilst the employment contract is still being performed, must be expressly stipulated,* either by the employment contract or by the collective bargaining agreement[93]. In addition, in the event of a mutual termination agreement being entered into by the employer and the employee, the timeframe within which the employer can release the employee from the non-compete obligation commences on the date of termination of the employment contract set out by the parties in the written agreement approved by the Labour Authorities *(Direction régionale des entreprises, de la concurrence, de la consommation, du travail et de l'emploi - DIRECCTE).*[94]

Moreover, it has recently been decided that the employer, in the case of a mutual termination agreement, can only be released from his duty to pay the employee financial compensation for the non-compete obligation if this is expressly provided for in the written termination agreement.[95]

Also, the Court of Cassation held in early 2015 that the employee must comply with their non-compete obligation even in the event their employer goes out of business. Indeed, with the non-compete obligation becoming effective upon termination of the employment contract, a company's subsequent cessation of activity neither releases the employee from performing their non-compete obligation[96] nor frees the employer from their obligation to pay financial compensation to the employee.[97]

The Court of Cassation has held that an employee who violates their non-compete obligation, even on a temporary basis, must refund the non-compete compensation to their former employer. They also risk having to pay damages as compensation for the harm suffered by their former employer. Furthermore, the new employer may be held liable if they hire an employee knowing that such employee is bound by a non-compete clause with a former employer. However, a judge in summary proceedings cannot order the new employer to dismiss the employee. The first employer could only obtain in summary proceedings an injunction to order the employee to cease working for a competitor, together with a penalty to be paid for each day of work in breach of the judge's order.

Even in the absence of a non-compete clause, unfair competition by an employee is prohibited under French law. The former employer can file an unfair competition claim under sections 1240 and 1241 of the French Civil Code against the former employee if the latter commits any act of unfair competition having caused it a loss and\or against the new employer if the employee is hired elsewhere.

---

93. Employment Chamber of the Court of Cassation, 11 Mar. 2015, *no. 13-22.257.*
94. Employment Chamber of the Court of Cassation, 29 Jan. 2014, *no. 12-22.116.*
95. Employment Chamber of the Court of Cassation, 4 Feb. 2015, *no. 13-25.451.*
96. Employment Chamber of the Court of Cassation, 21 Jan. 2015, *no. 13-26.374.*
97. Employment Chamber of the Court of Cassation, 21 Jan. 2015, *no. 13-26.374.*

20.4. CHECKLIST OF DOS AND DON'TS

– An employee must be granted non-compete compensation in return for their agreement to be bound by a non-compete clause.
– An employer cannot present all documents and information remitted to the works council as being confidential, without this being deemed as abusive.

21. IMPLEMENTATION OF WHISTLEBLOWING SYSTEMS

21.1. OVERVIEW OF WHISTLEBLOWING REGULATIONS

In response to US financial scandals (Enron and WorldCom), American lawmakers passed the Sarbanes-Oxley Act of 30 July 2002, which required that listed companies in the United States and their foreign subsidiaries set up a system whereby their employees can report accounting and financial wrongdoings.

In France, a whistleblowing system is defined as a 'system whereby employees, or any other person exercising an activity in the company, can inform the head of the company or, as the case may be, other persons designated for such purposes, of problems that may seriously affect its activity or result in it being held seriously liable'. Such systems can take the form of an employee hotline or a dedicated email address.

A recent law (no. 2016-1691) adopted on 9 December 2016 (known as the 'Sapin II law') provides for the obligation for companies with at least fifty employees to implement internal procedures in order to receive the alerts issued by their employees or occasional and external staff.

Prior to this 2016 law, guidelines were set out in a circular issued by the French Labour Minister[98] and in a recommendation issued by the French data protection authority, the *CNIL*.[99,100]

21.2. REQUIREMENTS FOR VALIDITY

21.2.1. Authorisation by the French Data Protection Authority (*CNIL*)

Employers wishing to set up a whistleblowing system have to comply with a number of requirements. The French data protection authority (*CNIL*) stated

---

98. Circ. DGT 2008/22 of 19 Nov. 2008 relating to codes of ethics, professional whistleblowing systems and in-house regulations, p. 15.
99. Recommendation No. 2005-305 of 8 Dec. 2005 amended by recommendation no. 2014-042 of 30 Jan. 2014.
100. Commission Nationale de l'Informatique et des Libertés.

that when such systems are automated, they constitute data processing that falls within the scope of section 25-I 4° of the law of 6 January 1978 as amended, and therefore certain formalities must be carried out with the French data protection authority. Since the adoption of the recommendation of 8 December 2005 introducing a single authorization no. AU-004 (*autorisation unique*), employers can file a simplified declaration with the *CNIL (déclaration simplifiée)*, which is simply a commitment to comply with the recommendation's terms and conditions. So, in order to ensure compliance and consequently benefit from the simplified procedure, employers must notably make sure that the contemplated system concerns one of the areas specifically mentioned in the recommendation in question.

However, if the contemplated whistleblowing system does not comply with the terms and conditions of the said recommendation (e.g., if the envisaged system is to cover areas that are not expressly listed in the said recommendation, such as intellectual property or conflicts of interest), employers have to seek and obtain specific authorization *(autorisation spécifique)* from the French data protection authority.

By a recommendation of 30 January 2014, the French data protection authority amended the recommendation of 2005 and extended the scope of whistleblowing systems that can benefit from the simplified declaration. By doing so, the French data protection authority has considerably simplified preliminary formalities, as the procedure is based only on declarations.

The simplified procedure now applies to whistleblowing systems that are implemented in order to comply with a legal obligation or a legitimate interest and its scope is no longer limited to finance, accounting, banking or the fight against corruption, but encompasses three new areas, specifically the fight against discrimination and harassment, health, hygiene and safety at work and protection of the environment.

21.2.2.   Other Conditions

In addition, in order to be valid, a whistleblowing system must satisfy a certain number of cumulative conditions:

– The employees must not be under an obligation to use the whistleblowing system. It must remain optional.
– The whistleblowing system is a complementary scheme and must not replace an employee's 'right to alert' which is addressed to the staff representative bodies (sections L. 2313-2 and L. 2131-1 of the French Labour Code).
– The individual at the company who is in charge of collecting and processing the whistleblowing reports must be precisely identified.

- The whistleblowers must identify themselves, however their identity will be treated confidentially by the organization in charge of managing the whistleblowing system. Exceptionally, the whistleblower's identity can be withheld under certain circumstances but in order for an anonymous alert to be considered and processed, its author wishing to remain anonymous must establish the seriousness of the alleged facts and sufficiently detail the factual findings.
- The absence of use of the whistleblowing system must not give rise to disciplinary measures against the employees.
- The French data protection authority lists those categories of data that can be collected and processed.
- The system must comply with all provisions of Law no. 78-17 of 6 January 1978 on data protection (*Loi informatique et libertés*).
- The system must provide sufficient security guarantees.

The courts can cancel a whistleblowing system that does not fulfil the required conditions and order the destruction of the collected data .[101] In addition, the Court of Cassation has held that the failure to comply with the preliminary formalities required by the French data protection authority renders the system and any information collected void.[102]

21.2.3.   Procedure for Implementation within the Company

The implementation of a whistleblowing system also requires that an information-consultation procedure be conducted with the works council in accordance with section L. 2323-47 of the French Labour Code, and the health and safety committee.[103]

Pursuant to section L. 1222-4 of the French Labour Code and the data protection law of 1978 (*Loi informatique et libertés*), employees must be personally informed that the company will be setting up a whistleblowing system.

21.3.   CHECKLIST OF DOS AND DON'TS

- Do not implement a compulsory whistleblowing system or a system whereby employees will be subject to disciplinary measures if they do not use the system.

---

101. *Tribunal de Grande Instance* of Nanterre, 19 Oct. 2007, *no. 06/06460*, Dassault Systèmes.
102. Employment Chamber of the Court of Cassation, 6 Apr. 2004, *no. 01-45.227*.
103. *Tribunal de Grande Instance* of Nanterre, 27 Dec. 2006, *no. 2006/02550*, Dupont de Nemours.

– Obtain authorization from the French data protection authority (*CNIL*) before implementing a whistleblowing system.
– Limit the scope of the whistleblowing system.
– Obtain the works council's opinion and inform employees.

22. PROHIBITION OF DISCRIMINATION IN THE WORKPLACE

22.1. OVERVIEW OF ANTI-DISCRIMINATION AND PROFESSIONAL EQUALITY LAWS

22.1.1. Legal Sources

Section L. 1132-1 of the French Labour Code which summarizes all prohibited discrimination has been further extended by successive laws.

22.1.2. Direct or Indirect Discrimination

Section L. 1132-1 of the French Labour Code prohibits direct as well as indirect discrimination.

22.1.3. Burden of Proof

Section L. 1134-1 of the French Labour Code stipulates that:

> an employee or an applicant for a job, internship or vocational training programme must present factual elements which could indicate that direct or indirect discrimination has occurred; the onus is then on the employer to prove that their actions were justified by objective elements void of any discrimination.

22.1.4. Sanctions

Where an employer is found by an employment tribunal to have discriminated unlawfully against an employee, the tribunal is empowered to do the following:

– Declare the discriminatory act as null and void (in particular, a dismissal on discriminatory grounds will be null and void and the employee will have the right to be reinstated, and receive back payment of any salary not received as a result of their dismissal); and
– Order the employer to pay compensation to the employee.

Employers have a general obligation to ensure appropriate working conditions for their employees. Employers may therefore be liable for the discriminatory acts of their employees provided those acts are carried out 'in the course of employment'. In essence, the employer is deemed to have committed the unlawful act of the employees. This is the case even if the act was done without the knowledge or approval of the employer.

From a criminal law standpoint, refusing to hire an employee, or disciplining or dismissing an employee, on discriminatory grounds are criminal offences and subject to up to three years' imprisonment and a fine of EUR 45,000 (section 225-2 of the French Criminal Code).

22.2. AGE DISCRIMINATION

22.2.1. Legal Sources

Age discrimination is prohibited by section L. 1132-1 of the French Labour Code.

22.2.2. Differences in Treatment Based on Age

However, different treatment based on age does not necessarily constitute discrimination if it is objectively and reasonably justified by a legitimate purpose, in particular to protect the health or safety of employees, to facilitate their professional integration, to ensure their employment, redeployment or compensation in case of loss of employment, and when the means to achieve this purpose are necessary and appropriate.

Such different treatment can consist in particular of (i) prohibiting access to employment or implementing special working conditions to ensure the protection of both young and older workers; (ii) setting a maximum recruitment age based on the training required for the position or the need to have completed a reasonable period of employment before retirement (section L. 1133-2 of the French Labour Code).

Both the French Court of Cassation and the European Court of Justice have ruled that a job protection plan providing for different dismissal indemnities depending on age was discriminatory.[104,105]

---

104. Employment Chamber of the Court of Cassation, 9 Oct. 2012, *no. 11-23.142.*
105. European Union Court of Justice, 6 Dec. 2012, *no. 152/11.*

22.3.   Discrimination Based on Race, Nation or Origin

22.3.1.   Legal Sources

Section L. 1132-1 of the French Labour Code prohibits discrimination based on race, ethnicity or genetic characteristics. Discrimination based on race is also prohibited by Article 2 of the law dated 27 May 2008 in terms of social protection, health, social advantages, education, access to goods and services or providing goods and services.

French labour law prohibits discrimination based on belonging (even if only presumably) to an ethnic group or nation.

22.3.2.   Racial Discrimination

Racial discrimination is qualified when an employer takes into consideration skin colour, language, accent or nationality of a job applicant or an employee to take any decision.

22.3.3.   Measures to Combat Racial Discrimination

To combat this type of discrimination, the practice of 'testing' is authorized by the French Criminal Code.

Likewise, according to section L. 1221-7 of the French Labour Code an employer can examine job applicants 'anonymous' resumes without the applicant's name, but showing only their education and work experience.

22.4.   Gender Discrimination and Sexual Harassment

Under the influence of EU law, sexual harassment is treated as discrimination based on gender.

22.4.1.   Gender Discrimination

Section L. 1132-1 of the French Labour Code prohibits sexual discrimination. Section L. 1142-1 of the French Labour Code stipulates that (i) job offers must not mention the sex or the marital status of potential applicants (ii) that no one can refuse to hire a person, transfer or terminate an employee's contract or refuse to renew an employment contract on grounds of the person's gender, marital status or the fact that they are pregnant and (iii) that the employer cannot take measures, in particular concerning remuneration, training, appointment, qualification, classification, promotion or transfer on grounds of the person's gender or the fact that they are pregnant. Likewise, it has been recommended by the French Labour Authorities that advertisements use both masculine and feminine endings or gender neutral words in job descriptions, followed by M/F.

Section L. 1142-2 of the French Labour Code allows some differences in treatment on grounds of the person's gender where gender is a genuine professional requirement for the position (for instance actors required for a female/male role, models required to present male/female clothes, etc.) provided that the objective is legitimate and the requirement proportionate. Special treatment given to women in connection with pregnancy or childbirth is permitted and cannot form the basis of a sex discrimination complaint by a man.

Infringement of male-female equality legislation is a criminal offence subject to up to three years' imprisonment and a fine of EUR 45,000.

22.4.2. Sexual Harassment

Section L. 1153-1 of the French Labour Code provides that *no employee must be subjected to either sexual harassment or acts deemed to constitute sexual harassment.*

Section L. 1153-2 of the French Labour Code protects job applicants and employees who refuse to be subject to such sexual harassment.

Witnesses of acts of sexual harassment are also protected pursuant to section L. 1153-3 of the French Labour Code.

Section L. 1153-4 of the French Labour Code states that any provision contrary to the above sections is null and void.

Furthermore, section L. 1153-5 of the French Labour Code provides that it is the responsibility of the head of the company to take all necessary measures to prevent sexual harassment from occurring and requires that the provisions of section 222-33 of the French Criminal Code are displayed at the workplace and also at the entrance of premises where hiring is undertaken. In a recent decision, the Court of Cassation has ruled that just the occurrence of harassment constitutes a breach of the employer's obligation of safety, even if the employer, once they had been given notice of the actions considered as harassment, had immediately put an end to them.[106] In practice, this means that even if harassment has ceased, the employee's claim that he has been constructively dismissed is not necessarily unjustified.

---

106. Employment Chamber of the Court of Cassation, 11 Mar. 2015, *no. 13-18.603.*

Section 222-33 of the French Criminal Code reiterates the definition provided in section L. 1153-1 and states that such acts are subject to two years' imprisonment and a fine of EUR 30,000.

Section L. 1153-6 of the French Labour Code states that '*any employee who engaged in sexual harassment can be subject to disciplinary action*'.

22.5. HANDICAP AND DISABILITY DISCRIMINATION

22.5.1. Sources

A law dated 2005 on equal rights and opportunities for people with a disability provides several measures, ranging from non-discrimination measures, positive measures and specific contributions, to help people with a disability to access the labour market.

Section L. 1132-1 of the French Labour Code prohibits discrimination against handicapped persons because of their disability or for a reason related to their disability which cannot be objectively justified.

However, differences in treatment are permissible when based on disability acknowledged by the occupational health doctor because of health or handicap and when differences in treatment are objective, necessary and appropriate.

Measures for disabled people (positive discrimination), provided in section L. 5213-6 of the French Labour Code do not constitute discrimination.

Furthermore, section L. 5212-2 of the French Labour Code states that in companies with more than twenty employees, the number of handicapped workers, disabled ex-servicemen and other specifically defined disabled persons in full- or part-time positions must represent 6% of the company's total workforce.

22.5.2. Measures of Protection

In order to comply with this obligation, employers benefit from the following options:

- Directly employ handicapped or disabled individuals.
- Take on handicapped or disabled persons for training.
- Subcontract certain work to specialized companies or organizations specialized in employing handicapped or disabled individuals.
- Apply a collective bargaining agreement or enter into an agreement with trade union representatives to set up an action plan in favour of handicapped and disabled individuals.
- Pay an annual contribution to the French association for the promotion of employment of handicapped and disabled individuals (*AGEFIPH*).

22.6.   RELIGIOUS DISCRIMINATION

Section L. 1132-1 of the French Labour Code prohibits discrimination based on religious convictions.

It should be remembered that the company rules and regulations may include provisions promoting the principle of neutrality within the company and limiting the extent to which employees can manifest their religious convictions (please refer to section 6.2.1).

An employer can prevent employees from wearing religious symbols for objective reasons without this qualifying as discrimination, particularly if this could cause potential problems with clients or creates health or safety risks.

In the so-called *'Baby-Loup'* case, a Muslim employee refused to take off her veil despite a clause in the nursery's company rules and regulations requiring that its employees comply with an obligation of secularity (*'obligation de laïcité'*) and neutrality. Her repeated refusal was sanctioned by her dismissal for gross misconduct.

On 19 March 2013, the Employment Chamber of the Court of Cassation[107] declared her dismissal to be null and void justifying its decision by the fact that employees working for employers in the private sector and which do not manage a public service are not subject to this obligation of secularity. The Court stated that in this case any restriction on religious freedom must be duly justified by the nature of the task to be performed, be in response to an essential requirement and proportionate to the pursued goal as required by section L. 1321-3 of the French Labour Code. In the Court's opinion, the clause provided for in the nursery's company rules and regulations did not fulfil the requirements under section L. 1321-3 of the French Labour Code and deemed the clause to be too imprecise.

The Plenary Assembly of the Court of Cassation,[108] further to the decision of the Paris Court of Appeal of 27 November 2013[109] approving the dismissal for gross misconduct, put an end to this controversy by ruling that the clause in question limiting religious freedom was sufficiently precise, justified and proportionate to the desired objective. The Court of Cassation therefore validated the employee's dismissal.

This French *'Baby-Loup'* case will be combined with a the recent Court of Justice of the European Union decision which held that an internal rule of an undertaking which prohibits the visible wearing of any political, philosophical or religious sign does not constitute direct discrimination.[110]

---

107. Employment Chamber of the Court of Cassation, 19 Mar. 2013, *no. 11-28.845*.
108. Plenary Assembly of the Court of Cassation, 25 Jun. 2014, *no. 13-28.369*.
109. Paris Court of Appeal, 27 Nov. 2013, *no. 13/02891*.
110. Court of Justice of the European Union, 14 Mar. 2017, *no. C-157/15*.

However, the European Court judged that, in the absence of such a rule, the willingness of an employer to take account of a customer's wish not to have the employer's services provided by a worker wearing an Islamic headscarf cannot be considered an occupational requirement that can rule out discrimination.[111]

22.7. PREGNANCY DISCRIMINATION

The French Labour Code prohibits employers from taking into consideration the fact that an employee or job applicant is pregnant. In this respect, the Court of Cassation has held that an employee, victim of both pregnancy discrimination and moral harassment, is entitled, upon proof of separate and distinct harm sustained, to double compensation.[112] In addition, pregnant women and women on maternity or adoption leave cannot be dismissed. An employee's employment contract is suspended while she is on maternity or adoption leave. The prohibition to dismiss such employees is, however (i) limited in time; and (ii) subject to exceptions (sections L. 1225-4 and L. 1225-5 of the French Labour Code).

22.7.1. Prohibition to Dismiss

Except as provided below, an employer cannot terminate the contract of a pregnant employee whose pregnancy has been medically acknowledged or of an employee on maternity leave.

If the above rule is violated, the dismissal is automatically null and void (section L. 1225-70 of the French Labour Code) if, within fifteen days of receiving notice of termination, the employee sends her employer, by registered mail with acknowledgement of receipt, a medical certificate proving that she is pregnant. A pregnant woman dismissed because of her pregnancy is entitled to damages for the loss incurred in addition to the dismissal indemnity and salary which would have paid during the whole period of protection (section L. 1225-71 of the French Labour Code).

If a company fails to comply with the provisions on maternity and adoption, they may be subject to fines of up to EUR 750 (section R. 1227-5 of the French Labour Code). Termination on the grounds of pregnancy is a criminal offence subject to up to three years' imprisonment and a fine of EUR 45,000 (section 225-2 of the French Criminal Code).

---

111. Court of Justice of the European Union, 14 Mar. 2017, *no. C-188/15.*
112. Employment Chamber of the Court of Cassation, 3 Mar. 2015, *no. 13-23.521.*

22.7.2.   Exceptions

It is permissible under French labour law to dismiss an employee who is pregnant if the employee has committed serious misconduct, or if it is impossible to continue the contract (section L. 1225-5 of the French Labour Code). The reason put forward by the employer to justify their decision must be unrelated to the fact that the employee is pregnant.

22.8.   MARITAL STATUS, SEXUAL ORIENTATION AND GENDER IDENTITY DISCRIMINATION

22.8.1.   Marital Status

An employer cannot refuse to hire or offer a promotion to an applicant or employee because of their family or marital situation.

22.8.2.   Sexual Orientation

It is prohibited to discriminate on the basis of an employee's sexual orientation notably in order to prevent homophobia.

For example, dismissal of a male employee wearing earrings without justifying that it undermines the legitimate interests of the company is discriminatory.[113]

22.8.3.   Gender Identity

Since the French Law of 6 August 2012 on sexual harassment, gender identity can constitute grounds for unlawful discrimination. This aims at protecting transsexuals or transgendered people, not from being discriminated against on the grounds of their gender or their sexual orientation, but because of their physical appearance that does not correspond to their civil status or because they have changed civil status.

22.9.   HOME LOCATION DISCRIMINATION

Since the French law dated 21 February 2014, an employer cannot refuse to hire or offer a promotion to an applicant or employee because of the location of such employee's home.

---

113. Employment Chamber of the Court of Cassation, 11 Jan. 2012.

In addition, pursuant to section L. 1133-5 of the French Labour Code, 'measures taken in favour of persons residing in certain geographical areas and measures aimed at promoting equal treatment' do not constitute discrimination.

22.10. TRADE UNION DISCRIMINATION

Pursuant to the general principle of non-discrimination, discrimination due to trade union activity or membership, either direct or indirect, is prohibited (section L. 1132-1 of the French Labour Code).

More specifically, section L. 2141-5 of the French Labour Code prohibits any employer from taking any discriminatory decision on grounds of union membership or activity.

Since the French law dated 17 August 2015, a trade union member, at the beginning of his mandate and at his request, may benefit from an individual interview regarding practical arrangements for exercising his trade union activity within the company. When a professional development interview (*entretien professionnel*) takes place at the end of the mandate, and under certain conditions, the skills acquired during the mandate can be noted and it can be discussed how the experience can be validated (section L. 2141-5 of the French Labour Code).

An employer must not take into consideration an employee's trade union activity, in any manner whatsoever, for their professional appraisal.[114]Such union activity must not impact in any manner whatsoever the employee's remuneration.

22.11. RETALIATION

Sections L. 1132-3 and L. 1132-4 of the French Labour Code protect victims or witnesses of discrimination from retaliation by their employer. Any disciplinary measure, dismissal or discriminatory action taken by an employer against an employee because the employee testified or took action in court is null and void. The employee does not have to prove that their allegations were true in order to benefit from this protection granted by law.

An employee cannot be dismissed because they complained about discrimination, even if this discrimination is finally deemed not to have existed.[115]

---

114. Employment Chamber of the Court of Cassation, 23 Mar. 2011, *no. 09-72.733.*
115. Court of Appeal, 7 Jul. 2011, *no. 10/00973.*

22.12.   CONSTRUCTIVE DISMISSAL

An employee who is repeatedly discriminated against by their employer is entitled to claim that they have been constructively dismissed. To claim compensation for unfair dismissal, the employee must prove that the facts are serious enough to constitute constructive dismissal.

22.13.   CHECKLIST OF DOS AND DON'TS

–   Do not take an employee's private life into consideration when making employment decisions.
–   Make employment decisions based on an objective assessment of the employee's skills and capabilities.

23.   SMOKING IN THE WORKPLACE

23.1.   OVERVIEW OF SMOKING BAN

Smoking is prohibited in all enclosed and covered work areas, whether for collective use (e.g., reception halls, company cafeterias and meeting rooms) or individual use (e.g., individual offices).

While not a requirement, an employer can set up smoking rooms after consulting the health and safety committee (CHSCT) or the staff delegates if there is no CHSCT, and the company doctor.

23.2.   SANCTIONS

Penalties for the violation of non-smoking rules are provided by sections R. 3515-2 and R. 3515-3 of the French Public Health Code, as follows:

–   third-class fine for individuals who violate non-smoking rules that is, up to EUR 450;
–   fourth-class fine for employers who fail to comply with their obligations in this regard, that is, up to EUR 750 for the legal representative and EUR 3,750 for the company.

The employer is bound by an absolute obligation in respect of the employees' work safety. Employers are required to take all necessary measures to ensure the security and protect the health of their employees, including protecting them in relation to the dangers of smoking. The French courts have acknowledged that there was constructive dismissal of an employee where the employer failed to comply with non-smoking rules.[116]

23.3. CHECKLIST OF DOS AND DON'TS

– Ensure that smoking is prohibited in the company.
– Provide smokers with specially designated smoking rooms.

24. USE OF DRUGS AND ALCOHOL IN THE WORKPLACE

24.1. OVERVIEW

Section R. 4228-20 of the French Labour Code prohibits all alcoholic drinks at the workplace other than wine, beer, cider and a specific pear-based liqueur.

24.2. TESTING

An employer cannot require employees to undergo alcohol or drug tests if the sole purpose is to monitor employees' ability to work.[117]

For the Supreme Court, testing must be justified by the dangers relating to the employee's duties and its results may be challenged by the employee; otherwise it is illegal.[118,119]

Alcohol testing must be expressly provided for in the company rules and regulations and in a recent decision, the Court of Cassation ruled that even if company rules and regulations provide for such a clause, only employees in an obvious state of drunkenness can be forced to undergo an alcohol test.[120]

24.3. CHECKLIST OF DOS AND DON'TS

– Impose a total ban on alcohol in the workplace only for specific hazardous situations.
– Conduct alcohol tests only if justified by the employee's duties (e.g., a truck driver or deliveryman) and if challenging the results is possible.

---

116. Employment Chamber of the Court of Cassation, 6 Oct. 2010, *no. 09-65.103.*
117. *Conseil d'Etat*, 1 Feb. 1980, *no. 06321.*
118. Employment Chamber of the Court of Cassation, 22 May 2002, *no. 99-45.878.*
119. Employment Chamber of the Court of Cassation, 24 Feb. 2004, *no. 01-47.000.*
120. Employment Chamber of the Court of Cassation, 2 Jul. 2014, *no. 13-13.757.*

25.   MATTERS RELATED TO HEALTH AND DISEASES SUCH AS AIDS, HIV, SARS, BLOODBORNE PATHOGENS

25.1.   OVERVIEW

A job applicant does not have to disclose health information to his future employer, and the future employer is not allowed to ask an applicant questions about their health.

Under French case law, a dismissal based on absences due to sick leave may be admitted under certain conditions.

25.2.   HEALTH DISCRIMINATION

Furthermore, pursuant to section L. 1132-1 of the French Labour Code, no one can be excluded from a recruitment procedure or from access to an internship or training programme, or be sanctioned, dismissed or subject to discriminatory action, directly or indirectly, because of health.

For example, justifying an employee's slow career development by frequent sick leave is discriminatory.[121]

However, sick leave may be taken into consideration in the calculation of a bonus based on assiduity without being discriminatory if all types of absence are taken into account.[122]

25.3.   AUTHORIZED DISMISSAL

An employer may dismiss an employee on grounds of health provided the employee's health results in (i) prolonged absence from work or repeated sick leave (ii) disrupting operations and damaging the proper running of the company (iii) so that such absences necessitate the permanent replacement of the employee.[123]

The employer may also dismiss an employee whose inability to work has been formally assessed by the occupational health doctor, subject to specific requirements and procedure.

---

121. Employment Chamber of the Court of Cassation, 28 Jan. 2010, *no. 08-44.486*; Employment Chamber of the Court of Cassation, 9 Apr. 2015, *no.* 13-27.095.
122. Employment Chamber of the Court of Cassation, 11 Jan. 2012, *no. 10-23.139.*
123. Employment Chamber of the Court of Cassation, 26 Jan. 2011, *no. 09-71.907* and *no. 09-67.073.*

25.4.   CHECKLIST OF DOS AND DON'TS

- Do not ask a job applicant questions regarding their medical history or current state of health.
- Do not take any decision vis-à-vis an employee based on health reasons.
- Only dismiss an employee due to their health when their replacement is necessary because their absence on sick leave disrupts the general running of the company.

26.   DRESS AND GROOMING REQUIREMENTS

26.1.   OVERVIEW

Freedom to dress as one wishes is not a fundamental freedom under French law.[124]

Freedom to dress as one wishes is subject to section L. 1121-1 of the French Labour Code prohibiting limitations on individual and collective rights or freedoms which are not justified by the nature of the task to be performed or proportional to the objective sought.

Even though it does not constitute a fundamental right, the courts have ruled that a dismissal is null and void if it is based on the refusal to comply with a dress code requirement deemed to be discriminatory.[125] In this case, the employer wanted to stop an employee from wearing earrings because he was a man.

26.2.   ADMITTED LIMITATIONS

As freedom to dress as one wishes does not constitute a fundamental right, an employer is therefore allowed to impose dress and grooming requirements on the employees if required by the position held by the employees concerned, or due to health and safety issues (e.g., in case of handling food or hazardous substances) or in the interest of the customer (e.g., for identification of a salesperson in a store).

An employer may require that its employees wear decent and clean clothes (e.g., prohibition to wear a sweat suit[126]).

---

124. Employment Chamber of the Court of Cassation, 28 May 2003, *no. 02-40.273.*
125. Employment Chamber of the Court of Cassation, 11 Jan. 2012, *no. 10.28.213.*
126. Employment Chamber of the Court of Cassation, 6 Nov. 2001, *no. 99-43.988.*

26.3.   CHECKLIST OF DOS AND DON'TS

– Impose dress rules only on objective grounds.

27.   PRIVACY, TECHNOLOGY AND TRANSFER OF PERSONAL DATA

27.1.   OVERVIEW

An employee has a right to privacy during work time and in the workplace.

If an employer wishes to monitor the employees' activity, the employer must first inform the employees and consult the works council. In case of automated processing of personal data, a preliminary declaration must be filed with the French data protection authority (*CNIL*).

27.2.   PRIVACY RIGHTS AND LIMITATIONS ON MONITORING

There are specific limitations on the extent to which employees can be monitored at work. In particular:

– Employees have the right to use IT equipment made available to them for personal purposes, provided that this use remains reasonable. As a general rule all documents in the employee's office or computer files are presumed to be professional, and the employer may therefore access them without the employee's permission or presence. However, although the employer is the owner of the computer used by the employee to perform their work, as a general rule, an employer cannot consult any computer files that the employee has marked as personal. This prohibition is waived in case of overriding reasons, provided that the employee has been duly informed of the employer's intention and insofar as they had the opportunity to be present when the files were viewed.
– The employer must respect the employee's right to privacy relating to correspondence, and may not open emails sent or received by the employee at the workplace if it is marked as personal.
– Employees have the right to use company-provided telephones for personal purposes, provided that this use remains reasonable. Employers have the right to check the telephone numbers called without having to inform the employees that they are doing so. However, in order to listen to telephone conversations, the employer must expressly inform employees as provided above. The Court of Cassation has ruled that text messages sent or received by a mobile phone made available to the employee by the employer to

carry out their tasks are presumed to be professional. As a consequence, the employer is legally entitled to consult these text messages without the employee's presence, unless the messages are marked as personal.[127]
– An employer who accesses emails sent and received from an employee's personal email account violates the secrecy of correspondence, even if these messages were written on the employee's work computer.[128]

27.3. CHECKLIST OF DOS AND DON'TS

– Respect the employee's private life at the workplace.
– Inform the employees and consult the works council if any systems are to be put in place for monitoring their activity or personal data.
– Distinguish between professional and personal files and emails.

28. WORKPLACE INVESTIGATIONS FOLLOWING COMPLAINTS OF DISCRIMINATION, HARASSMENT, FRAUD, THEFT AND WHISTLEBLOWING

28.1. OVERVIEW

As owner of the company's assets, an employer is entitled to control and oversee the employees' activity. This right is limited, however, by the employees' right to privacy, even during work time and at their place of work.

28.2. RIGHT TO CONTROL

This right is recognized by French case law and is based on the principle of loyalty when searching for evidence. In particular, the works council must be informed and consulted on the means and the techniques used to control the activity of the employees before the decision is made to implement these means and techniques in the company (section L. 2323-6 of the French Labour Code).

Employees must be informed of any 'video surveillance' systems that are implemented on work premises.

In case of automated processing via name-specific information, a preliminary declaration must be filed with the French data protection authority (*CNIL*), the

---

127. Commercial Chamber of the Court of Cassation, 10 Feb. 2015, *no. 13-14.779.*
128. Employment Chamber of the Court of Cassation, 26 Jan. 2016, *no. 14-15.368* and 7 April 2016, *no. 14-27.949.*

works council must be consulted and the employees must be able to obtain a copy of the information concerning them.

Any monitoring that the employer intends to apply in order to have disciplinary power over the employees must be declared both to the employees and to the *CNIL*. Failure to comply with these requirements will prevent the employer from applying disciplinary sanctions on this basis.[129]

28.3.   CHECKLIST OF DOS AND DON'TS

- Consult with the works council before implementing any tools or techniques designed to monitor the employees' activity.
- In the event of any automated monitoring scheme, inform the employees, consult the works council and file a declaration with the *CNIL*.

29.   AFFIRMATIVE ACTION/NON-DISCRIMINATION REQUIREMENTS

29.1.   OVERVIEW

French law contains few positive discrimination provisions. Pursuant to section L. 5212-2 of the French Labour Code, handicapped employees must make up 6% of the workforce in companies that usually employ at least twenty employees. Section L. 1142-4 of the French Labour Code authorizes equal opportunity programmes for women in order to rectify de facto unequal treatment. These catch-up measures are temporary.

The French legislator has also imposed obligations requiring companies with at least 50 employees to negotiate an agreement with regard to equality between male and female employees and employment of older people (replaced by the 'generation contract' provided by Section L. 5121-6 of the French Labour Code).

29.2.   PROFESSIONAL EQUALITY BETWEEN MALE AND FEMALE EMPLOYEES

Further to the law of 17 August 2015, existing bargaining topics are divided into three major negotiating themes. Professional equality between male and

---

129.   Employment Chamber of the Court of Cassation, 8 Oct. 2014, *no. 13-14.991.*

female employees is now a negotiating theme. Unless the company has already concluded a collective agreement specifically on professional equality between male and female employees, employers must initiate each year a negotiation process on goals regarding professional equality between male and female employees present within the company and the measures aimed at achieving these targets (sections L. 2242-1 and L. 2242-8 of the French Labour Code). In the absence of a collective agreement, the employer must instead draw up an action plan (*plan d'action*) to ensure professional equality between women and men. After evaluating the objectives and measures taken during the past year, this action plan, based on clear criteria, specific and operational objectives determines the goals for the coming year, defines qualitative and quantitative actions to reach the goals, and assesses their costs. This action plan is filed with the Labour Authority. A summary of the action plan, including at least the indicators of progress and goals, is displayed at the workplace to be brought to attention of employees. It is also made available for anyone who requests it and it is published on the company's website, if it has one.

The absence of a collective agreement or an action plan may result in the company being ordered to pay a maximum fine of 1% of the monthly wage bill. This penalty must be paid for each full month during which the company is not covered by an agreement or an action plan (section L. 2242-9 of the French Labour Code).

29.3. OLDER EMPLOYEES AND THE 'GENERATION CONTRACT'

Under sections L. 5121-6 et seq. of the French Labour Code, a new scheme has been implemented, aimed at establishing junior-senior working partnerships, ensuring employment of young people while keeping older people in employment and ensuring the transfer of knowledge and skills.

Since 30 September 2013, all companies must implement, every three years, an in-house collective agreement concerning the 'generation contract'. If companies fail to enter into an in-house agreement, they will be subject to a financial penalty. More precisely, prior to a law of 5 March 2014, companies and groups of between 50 and less than 300 employees could only obtain financial aid regarding the 'generation contract' if they entered into an intergenerational collective agreement or were covered by an 'action plan' (*plan d'action*). With the law of 5 March 2014, the legislator removed this obligation: hence, these companies and groups can receive financial aid upon conclusion of a 'generation contract' meeting all the conditions set out in the French Labour Code. However, companies and groups failing, for instance, to enter into an in-house agreement, industry-wide agreement or action plan, are subject to financial penalties.

29.4.   CHECKLIST OF DOS AND DON'TS

- Ensure that equal opportunity programmes for women are temporary.
- Take concrete measures to employ older employees.
- Comply with obligation of negotiating collective bargaining agreements relating to male and female equality and older employees.

30.   RESOLUTION OF DISCRIMINATION, EMPLOYMENT AND LABOUR DISPUTES: LITIGATION, ARBITRATION, MEDIATION AND CONCILIATION

30.1.   OVERVIEW

Alternative dispute resolution is not common practice in France. In the event of a dispute, the matter is usually referred to the courts. Nevertheless, certain provisions of the French Labour Code and, more widely, a law dated 8 February 1995 on the organization of the courts and civil procedure, provide for alternative dispute resolution procedures.

Collective labour disputes such as strikes may be resolved by various means other than judicial proceedings, such as arbitration, mediation and conciliation which constitute alternative dispute resolution.

Individual employment disputes between employers and employees are referred to the relevant employment tribunal (*conseil de prud'hommes*).

30.2.   ALTERNATIVE DISPUTE RESOLUTION PROCESSES FOR COLLECTIVE LABOUR DISPUTES

30.2.1.   New Participatory Proceedings

Conciliation is an optional alternative dispute resolution method for collective labour disputes whereby the parties try to reach a mutually acceptable settlement of their dispute via a third party (sections L. 2522-1 et seq. of the French Labour Code). Conciliation takes place before a commission consisting of three members representing employees, employers and the State. The State representative has the responsibility of trying to obtain that the two parties reach a settlement. Where conciliation fails, the dispute may be referred to mediation or arbitration (section L. 2522-6 of the French Labour Code). This type of conciliation process must not be confused with the initial attempt at conciliation before the employment tribunal, where the judges first try to obtain that the parties reach an out-of-court agreement to settle their dispute (please refer to 30.3.2).

Mediation is another alternative dispute resolution method (sections L. 2523-1 et seq. of the French Labour Code) which may be implemented in case of failure of the above conciliation or upon request. Once the designated mediator has collected all of the information relating to the dispute, they will submit a recommendation to the parties within one month as to how to resolve the dispute. Unlike the conciliator, the mediator has certain powers (to make enquiries, seek expert opinions, etc.). The recommendation is not binding, and the parties have eight days to reject it.

30.2.2. Arbitration

Arbitration is an optional alternative dispute resolution method for collective labour disputes whereby the parties entrust an arbitrator to take a decision either at law or in equity with regard to the dispute (sections L. 2524-1 et seq. of the French Labour Code). Recently, there have been instances of arbitration being used for individual labour disputes.

30.3. LITIGATION

30.3.1. Courts Having Jurisdiction in Employment and Labour-Related Matters

The employment tribunal (*conseil de prud'hommes*) is a tribunal composed of elected judges, including an equal number of employee and employer representatives (section L. 1421-1 of the French Labour Code). The employment tribunal has jurisdiction to hear all individual disputes between employees and employers in respect of employment contracts (section L. 1411-3 of the French Labour Code).

As from 2017, judges will no longer be elected but rather from lists drawn up by the trade unions and representative employers' organizations at a national level, as stated in Ministerial Order no. 2016-388 of 31 March 2016.

The *Tribunal de Grande Instance*, a civil law court, has jurisdiction to hear all collective employment disputes, in particular in respect of collective negotiations and strikes.

Pursuant to Article R. 2314-27 of the French Labour Code, the *tribunal d'instance*, another civil law court, has jurisdiction to hear matters concerning electoral law and elections in the workplace.

30.3.2. Proceedings before the Employment Tribunal

Conciliation is a compulsory preliminary phase in proceedings before the employment tribunal (*conseil des prud'hommes*) (section L. 1411-1 of the French Labour Code). At the conciliation hearing, the judge will attempt to resolve the dispute by acting in a similar way to a mediator, rather than actually judging the case.

In the context of the conciliation proceedings, the judges can order certain measures, such as the production of documents (pay slips, working certificates), the provisional payment of salary or the payment of an indemnity (limited to six months of salary) and preliminary investigations.

There is no conciliation phase in certain circumstances, such as when there has been alleged infringement of an individual's freedoms in the workplace, requalification of a fixed-term contract as an indefinite-term contract, salary due in the event of insolvency or receivership and summary judgment claims.

If the parties' attempt at conciliation fails, the conciliation proceedings are then converted into judgment proceedings.

Pursuant to section L. 1235-1 of the French Labour Code, disputes may be settled in the conciliation phase by agreement between the parties. Such agreement provides for a lump-sum indemnity to be paid by the employer to the employee. The amounts are determined as follows[130]:

- two months' salary if the employee has less than one year of length of service;
- three months' salary if the employee has a length of service of at least one year, to which is added one month of salary per additional year of length of service up to eight years;
- ten months' salary if the employee has a length of service of between eight years and less than twelve years;
- twelve months' salary if the employee has a length of service of between twelve years and less than fifteen years;
- fourteen months' salary if the employee has a length of service of between fifteen years and less than nineteen years;
- sixteen months' salary if the employee has a length of service of between nineteen years and less than twenty-three years;
- eighteen months' salary if the employee has a length of service of between twenty-three years and less than twenty-six years;
- twenty months' salary if the employee has a length of service of between twenty-six years and less than thirty years;
- twenty-four months' salary if the employee has a length of service of more than thirty years.

---

130. Section D. 1235-21 of the French Labour Code.

In exchange, the employee would undertake to waive all pending claims. In cases in which the total amount of one of the party's claims does not exceed EUR 4,000 or if the claimant has requested an employment certificate, payslip or any other document that the employer is required to deliver to the employee, the employment tribunal's decision is final and cannot be appealed against. It may only be reviewed by the Court of Cassation.

In cases involving claims of EUR 4,000 or more, the employment tribunal's decision can be appealed against before a Court of Appeal.

A new French law published on 19 November 2016[131] provides for the possibility for registered associations and for associations that have been duly declared for at least five years to launch a class action before the *Tribunal de Grande Instance* in the following specific fields:

- discrimination;[132]
- health;[133]
- environment;[134]
- data protection.[135]

More specifically, class actions for breach of laws on discrimination should be brought by a trade union or an association duly declared for at least five years and involved in the fight against discrimination or in the field of disability[136]. Such class action may seek to obtain compliance with the law and, if appropriate, payment of damages[137].

30.3.3.   Statute of Limitations

According to the French Labour Code, the statutes of limitation are the following:

- The limitation period for claims related to performance or termination of the employment contract is two years from the date on which the employee had knowledge or should have had knowledge of facts enabling them to exercise their right, except for any specific statute of limitations (e.g., validity of an economic dismissal procedure, discrimination, moral harassment) (section L. 1471-1 of the French Labour Code).
- The limitation period for claims relating to salary payments is three years from the date on which the employee had knowledge or should have had

---

131. Law no. 2016-1547 on modernisation of justice (*Loi de modernisation de la justice du XXIeme siècle*).
132. Sections L. 1134-6 et seq. of the French Labour Code.
133. Sections L. 1143-1 et seq. of the French Public Health Code.
134. Sections L. 142-3-1 et seq. of the French Environmental Code.
135. Section 43*ter* of the law on data protection (*Loi informatique et libertés*).
136. Section L. 1134-7 of the French Labour Code.
137. Section L. 1134-8 of the French Labour Code.

knowledge of facts enabling them to exercise their right (section L. 3245-1 of the French Labour Code).

30.3.4.   Settlement Agreement

A settlement agreement may be entered into between the parties in order to settle a dispute (sections 2044 to 2049 of the French Civil Code).A settlement agreement must meet the following criteria in order to be enforceable and valid:

– The settlement agreement must be concluded after the occurrence of the dispute, in particular after the notification of a dismissal in case of a dispute regarding the termination of the employment contract at the employer's initiative;
– Each party must agree to reciprocal and real concessions;
– A settlement agreement must include undertakings by both parties to waive all claims, and consideration for doing so paid by the employer.

In addition, the employer and the employee are free to enter into a settlement agreement after the conclusion of a mutual termination agreement. Nevertheless, the Court of Cassation considers that: (i) the settlement agreement may only be entered into after the Labour Authorities has approved the mutual termination agreement, and (ii) the settlement agreement must not concern a dispute relating to a breach of the employment contract.[138]

Settlement agreements are binding res judicata, and can only be overturned if it is found that no consideration was paid for the employee's waiver of claims. The Court of Cassation confirmed a settlement agreement's res judicata nature by ruling that such an agreement, drafted in general terms and entered into after the termination of the employment contract prevents an employee from claiming salary back pay before the Labour Court.[139]

30.4.   CHECKLIST OF DOS AND DON'TS

– Although litigation is still typically used when there is a dispute with an employer, depending on the nature of the specific case (collective labour dispute or individual employment litigation), it may be advisable to try to resolve the dispute through an alternative dispute resolution procedure.

---

138. Employment Chamber of the Court of Cassation. 26 Mar. 2014 *no. 12-21.136 and* 25 Mar. 2015 *no. 13-23.368.*
139. Employment Chamber of the Court of Cassation, 5 Nov. 2014, *no 13-18.984.*

31. EMPLOYER RECORDKEEPING, DATA PROTECTION AND EMPLOYEE ACCESS TO PERSONAL DATA AND RECORDS

31.1. OVERVIEW

The French data protection law of 1978 (*loi informatique et libertés*) governs the automated and non-automated processing of personal data. Employers who wish to implement a personal data processing system must obtain prior authorization from the French data protection authority (*CNIL*).

31.2. DATA PROTECTION RULES

Any collection, processing and storage of data related to employees must be for legitimate and determined purposes, and must be proportional to the objective pursued. Data can only be kept for a limited period of time which depends on the type of data at issue. Pursuant to sections L. 1221-9 and L. 1222-4 of the French Labour Code, employees must be informed of any collection, processing and storage of data concerning them, and the employer must file a declaration with the French data protection authority (*CNIL*) prior to commencing collection, processing or storage.

Any automated processing of personal data which could potentially violate an employee's rights and freedom must first be submitted to the French data protection authority (*CNIL*) for authorization.

31.3. EMPLOYEE ACCESS TO PERSONAL DATA

Employees have a right to access data concerning them, and to obtain that their employer rectify or delete incomplete, ambiguous or out-of-date data, or data whose collection, use, communication or storage is prohibited.

31.4. CRIMINAL SANCTIONS

The failure to file the aforementioned declarations with the French data protection authority (*CNIL*) is subject to up to five years of imprisonment and a fine of up to EUR 300,000 for the representative of the company and/or a fine of up to EUR 1,500,000 for the company (section 226-16 of the French Criminal Code). This is in addition to any additional fines that may be ordered by the French data protection authority (*CNIL*).

The disclosure of information to non-authorized persons is subject to up to five years of imprisonment and a fine of up to EUR 300,000 for the representative of the company and/or a fine of up to EUR 1,500,000 for the company. Where the disclosure of information is due to carelessness or negligence, it is subject to up to three years of imprisonment and a fine of up to EUR 100,000 (section 226-22 of the French Criminal Code).

Refusing or hindering the exercise of the employees' right to access and rectify data is subject to a EUR 1,500 fine per offence, and a EUR 3,000 fine for repeated offences (section 131-13 of the French Criminal Code).

32. REQUIRED NOTICES, POSTINGS AND UNION BOARDS

32.1. OVERVIEW OF REQUIRED NOTICES

Employers must display on a notice board in the workplace certain information, including notably:

– The name, address and telephone number of the relevant labour inspector.
– The address and telephone number of the occupational health doctor and of emergency services.
– The company rules and regulations.
– Criminal law provisions relating to non-discrimination, sexual and moral harassment.
– Instructions in case of a fire and a summary of instructions in the event of an electrical accident.
– The terms and conditions for telecommuting.
– Electoral notices.
– Mandatory profit-sharing.

32.2. UNION MESSAGES

– Pursuant to section L. 2142-3 of the French Labour Code, trade unions are allowed to post union related messages or flyers on specially designated bulletin boards. The trade union must give the employer a copy of the message at the time of posting.
– If an employer believes that a union message contains illegal content, summary proceedings before a judge must be commenced in order to have the message removed from the bulletin board. If the employer removes the message, this would constitute the criminal offence of obstruction.[140]

32.3. CHECKLIST OF DOS AND DON'TS

– Employers must display certain information at the premises.
– Employers must provide specific notice boards for trade union messages.

---

140. Criminal Chamber of the Court of Cassation, 19 Feb. 1979.